THE
LAST DAYS OF JESUS

THE
LAST DAYS OF JESUS

*

*The appearances of our Lord during the
forty days between the Resurrection and Ascension.*

*

T. V. MOORE, D. D.

THE BANNER OF TRUTH TRUST

THE BANNER OF TRUTH TRUST
3 Murrayfield Road, Edinburgh EH12 6EL
P O Box 621, Carlisle, Pennsylvania 17013, USA

*

First published 1858
First Banner of Truth edition 1981
ISBN 0 85151 321 2

*

Printed in U.S.A. by
Dickinson Brothers, Inc.
Grand Rapids, Michigan

CONTENTS

INTRODUCTION . . . . *ix*

CHAPTER 1
THE DARK HOUR BEFORE THE DAWN.

The Picture—The Smitten Flock—Keeping the Sabbath—the Darkness
ever before the Dawn 13

CHAPTER 2
THE DAWN.

The rising from the dead not recorded—Why? The resurrection not witnessed by any mortal eye—Advantage to us of this arrangement—The
dawn of the great morning 17

CHAPTER 3
THE ANGELIC ANNUNCIATION.

The great morning—The early visit—The angelic annunciation. I. *The
proof of the resurrection*. The empty tomb—The dilemma—The evidence complete. II. *The importance of the resurrection*. It set God's
seal to the Messiahship of Christ—It declared him divine—It opened
the dark valley—Its connection with justification, regeneration, holiness, and comfort to the sorrowing—The light cast on the believer's
grave from the place where the Lord lay 21

CHAPTER 4
THE FIRST APPEARANCE—LOVE WEEPING AT THE SEPULCHRE.

The first appearance, why to Mary Magdalene—The order of events—
The unspoken name—The two words—"Touch me not"—The broth-
er's message. I. *The spiritual mourner*. The cause of spiritual gloom—
The cure—The test—Rabboni. II. *The natural mourner*. The bereaved
—The disappointed—The fearful—The cure of all earthly sorrow. . 30

CHAPTER 5
THE SECOND APPEARANCE—OBEDIENCE REWARDED.

Order of events. Lessons from the second appearance. (1) *The mission of
woman*. Why the women were selected to tell the first tidings of the
resurrection—They do so still—Augustine, Alfred, Hall, Halyburton,
Doddridge, Wesley, Randolph, the convicted infidel—a mother's
power. (2) *The salutation of Jesus*. Blessings met only in the path of
obedience. (3) *Jesus worshipped*. Why Mary Magdalene was forbidden

what was allowed to the other women—The Divinity of Christ. (4) *The brotherly appellation*. The new name—The elder brother. (5) *The brotherly message*. Why meet in Galilee—The great appointment—Be ye also ready.

. . . . 40

CHAPTER 6

THE THIRD APPEARANCE—THE PENITENT BACKSLIDER.

The graduation—Why appear first to Peter? I. *The successive steps of the backslider*. (1) An unsubdued will. (2) Undue self-confidence. (3) Neglect of prayer. (4) Neglect of warnings. (5) Following Christ afar off. (6) Tampering with temptation—The avalanche. II. *The sorrows of the backslider*. The look in the palace and the bitter weeping—The backslider's musings—The starless crown. III. *The restoration of the backslider*. The three steps—Penitence, Hope, Assurance—The two kinds of repentance.

. . . . 49

CHAPTER 7

THE FOURTH APPEARANCE—THE PERPLEXED DOUBTERS.

The gradation. I. *The circumstances*. The sad disciples—The love of Jesus—The sin of unbelief—The key of the Old Testament—The burning of heart—Christ made known in breaking of bread. II. *The lessons to the doubter*. (1) Honest doubts in regard to the Divine origin of Christianity—"It speaks to my heart." (2) Doubts concerning doctrines. (3) Doubts regarding personal experience. (4) Doubts in reference to the Providential dealings of God. "Abide with us."

. . . . 57

CHAPTER 8

THE FIFTH APPEARANCE—THE LORD'S DAY EVENING.

The circumstances of this meeting—The physical properties of Christ's risen body. I. *The inauguration of the Lord's Day*. The Lord's day is the Christian Sabbath—Its beautiful significance. II. *The blessings connected with the Lord's Day by the words of Jesus*. (1) Fears relieved —Why do we dread a spirit?—"Peace." (2) Faith confirmed— Evidences of the resurrection—Transubstantiation. (3) Light cast on the objects of hope—The same body that dies rises—The physical properties of the risen body—Recognition in heaven. (4) Errors corrected. (5) The Holy Ghost given. (6) Apostolic power. III. *Thomas absent*. Why? — What he missed—Missing at the last.

. . . . 67

CHAPTER 9

THE SIXTH APPEARANCE—THE SCEPTICAL DISCIPLE.

The second Lord's day—The dark disciple—I. *The causes of the scepticism of Thomas*. (1) The original structure of his nature—Living in the shadow. (2) A wrong standard of belief—The credulity of unbelief. (3)

Absence from the meeting of the disciples—God honours his appointed means. II. *The consequence of his unbelief.* Wretchedness of soul —The sceptic wretched, whether right or wrong. III. *The removal of his scepticism.* (1) The awaking of his faith by a sight of Christ. (2) The confession of his faith—Did he blaspheme? (3) The personal character of his faith. (4) The benediction of Jesus—Goethe. 78

CHAPTER 10

THE SEVENTH APPEARANCE—THE SHORE OF GALILEE.

How the third meeting. I. *The circumstances.* The fishing party—The night of unsuccessful toil—The morning vision—The fire on the shore and the food. II. *The meaning of this scene.* The picnic interpretation—Connection with the first miraculous draught of fishes—The meaning of the first miracle—"Toiling all night and taking nothing" —The inefficiency of the pulpit—The difference of the miracles and their meaning—The second miracle shadows the final glory of the Church—The repast on the shore, its meaning—Lessons to the Church now on the sea—Comfort to the individual Christian 89

CHAPTER 11

THE SEVENTH APPEARANCE—LOVEST THOU ME ?

Peter reinvested with the apostolic office—The fire of coals. I. *The Questions.* (1) The name by which Peter was addressed. (2) The two words for love. (3) The contrast with the other disciples. (4) The gradual relenting of Jesus to Peter. II. *The charges.* Feeding and governing the flock—No primacy of Peter here—The girding of old age. III. *Lessons from this scene.* (1) The essence of the Christian life is love to Christ. (2) The test of love is obedience—The German pastor and the picture. (3) Love to Christ is made perfect through suffering—The girdings and carryings of the Christian—Not loving Christ—Maranatha. 100

CHAPTER 12

THE SEVENTH APPEARANCE—WHAT IS THAT TO THEE ?

The walk on the shore—Silent love—uncertainty of tradition—The breathing grave. I. *The question.* Peter's possible motives. (1) A momentary pang of repining—The feelings of the afflicted—A target for the Almighty. (2) Mere curiosity—Intimacy of Peter and John— Anxiety to pry into the future—Wisdom of the veil that hides it. II. *The answer.* (1) The events of life ordered by the will of God—Predestination a doctrine full of comfort. (2) The Christian's life on earth is a tarrying for the summons home—The aged and invalid—The Dairyman's Daughter. (3) The cure of all anxiety for the future is the discharge of present duty—Follow Jesus. 111

CHAPTER 13

THE EIGHTH APPEARANCE—THE FIVE HUNDRED WITNESSES.

I. *Place of this meeting.* Probably the mount of transfiguration—Why in Galilee. II. *Importance of this meeting.* Thrice predicted—A meeting of the whole church then on earth—Preparation for coming conflicts by a revelation of Christ's glory—Why some doubted. III. *Comparative silence of scripture concerning it.* Reason for this silence—The transfiguration. why so little alluded to—Meeting Jesus on earth—Meeting him hereafter in heaven. 120

CHAPTER 14

THE NINTH APPEARANCE—JAMES THE LORD'S BROTHER.

The three Jameses—James the Just, the brother of our Lord—His character by Hegesippus—Apocryphal traditions—His childhood and Nazaritic dedication—Not a disciple of Jesus at first—His position in the church—The significance of this appearance to him—The silence of scripture—General teachings. 127

CHAPTER 15

THE TENTH APPEARANCE—THE APOSTOLIC COMMISSION IN MATTHEW.

The place Jerusalem and Olivet—The four forms of the commission—Why?—Their distinctness—Meaning of the commission—Not the original authority to preach and baptize. I. *Authority* of the commission. The mediatorial kingdom of Christ—All power. II. *The commission.* (1) To make disciples (2) To baptize disciples—Subject of baptism—Baptismal formula—Trinity. (3) To teach disciples—Inspiration—The three offices of Christ. III. *Encouragement.* The presence of Christ—I AM—"All days"—Days of worship, of toil, of trial, and of death. . 134

CHAPTER 16

THE TENTH APPEARANCE—APOSTOLIC COMMISSION IN MARK.

The difference between Matthew and Mark, just such as we would expect—The Roman gospel. I. *The commission.* Its extent—Are infants excluded from baptism by its terms?—The illogical inference—Why infants are not named in the commission—The real warrant of the commission. II. *The authenticating seals.* The miracles of the soul. III. *The consequences of accepting or rejecting.* The awful words—Eternity the only interpreter. 151

CHAPTER 17

THE TENTH APPEARANCE—APOSTOLIC COMMISSION IN LUKE.

Differences between Luke and the other evangelists—The Greek gospel. I. *The Holy Scripture the only final and unerring rule of faith and practice.* Popery and infidelity—Jesus endorsing the scripture. II. *The*

central doctrine of revelation, an atoning and suffering Messiah. The
law, prophets, and psalms—The cross of Christ the centre of all
human history. III. *A divine power needful to enable man to comprehend the gospel of Christ.* "Opening the understanding"—The new
light. IV. *The salvation of the gospel for all, however remote their
habitation, or great their guilt.* "All nations"—Beginning at Jerusalem"—Bunyan's Jerusalem Sinner. 158

CHAPTER 18

THE TENTH APPEARANCE—APOSTOLIC COMMISSION IN ACTS.

The gospel of the Holy Ghost. I. *Waiting for the promise of the Father.*
Gorgeous dreams of the kingdom—Curiosity about the future—
Almanac makers of prophecy—Waiting for the vision—Creation
groaning—How must we wait? II. *The promise of the Father.* Meaning
of baptism—Mode of baptism—The dispensation of the Spirit
—Christ's ascent the condition of the Spirit's descent—Intercession of
the Holy Ghost, how it differs from that of Christ. III. *Effects of the
fulfilment of the promise.* All Christians witnesses for Christ—Passive
witnessing — Martyrs—Cecil and his mother, Addison — The unconscious witness. 168

CHAPTER 19

THE ASCENSION.

Why the Ascension is so little alluded to in scripture. I. *The fact of the
Ascension.* (1) The time. (2) The place. (3) The attendant circumstances. II. *The reasons for the Ascension.* (1)The Priesthood of Christ.
(2) The entrance into glory after suffering. (3) To display his Divine
nature. (4) Connection with the descent of the Holy Ghost. (5) His
intercession. (6) Preparing a place for us. (7) Our forerunner and
example—His Ascension the picture and pledge of ours. (8) Sitting at
the right hand of God—The Pilgrim 181

CHAPTER 20

THE PARTING PROMISE.

The lingering benediction. I. *The appearance of the Angels.* Angelic
agency—Its reality and blessedness—Its nature. II. The *Angelic Message.* (1) The rebuke—Gazing too long into heaven—"Oh! to be wi'
thee, Richie!"—Pining sinfully for heaven. (2) The comfort—"This
same Jesus"—The unchanging Friend. (3) The warning—The second
coming of Christ—The Old Testament Prophets—The New Testament
Prophets—Why such obscurity around the time and manner of this
coming—The great Epiphany—Conclusion—The fulness of instruction during the forty days—The coming Era—Signs of the times—The
Pentecost of the future. 198

INTRODUCTION

The number forty occurs so often in Scripture, especially in designating time, that we can hardly suppose this occurrence to be merely accidental. Especially is this true of the period of forty days. In the Patriarchal Dispensation, the flood was forty days in reaching its height, and forty days in abating. In the opening of the Legal Dispensation, Moses spent forty days in the Holy Mount before he came forth to deliver the law to the people. At this period the number appears with great frequency in designations of years. The life of Moses was included in three periods of forty years each; the people wandered in the desert for forty years; and the public life of Joshua began at the age of forty years. There would seem to be a period of forty days, just preceding the entrance into Canaan. We learn from Deut. 1. 3, compared with ch. 31. 2, and 34. 7, that Moses died the day he was one hundred and twenty years old, the first day of the eleventh month; and that the people mourned for him thirty days. We learn from Joshua 4. 19, that they passed through the Jordan, and entered Canaan on the tenth day of the first month. Hence there must have been precisely forty days interval between the end of the days of mourning for Moses, and the entrance into the land of Canaan under Joshua. When we reach the great representative of the prophetic era, Elijah, we find him led for forty days in the wilderness of Horeb. Ezekiel was required to bear the iniquity of Israel forty days, and forty days were granted to guilty Nineveh for repentance. At the opening of the New Testament, we meet it again in the duration of the fast and temptation of Jesus in the wilderness. And as his public ministry opened with this period of forty days, so it closes with the great forty days that elapsed between the resurrection and ascension, the most wonderful of them all.

It is perhaps impossible for us to understand all the reasons for the re-appearance of a particular number in this way. The mystical conjectures, and extravagant fancies of recent German writers show how easy it is to wander in the mist, and mistake a cloud for a crag, when we give loose to mere fancy in explaining facts. But there is at least one thing that is common to nearly all these periods of forty days. They were periods of preparation. The first forty days of Noah introduced the first great display of God's wrath that was made to the world. The second ushered in the second great chapter of human history, the dealings of God with the race of man since the flood. The forty days of Moses prepared him for setting up his Divine Institute. The forty days on the banks of Jordan, prepared Israel for their entrance into the promised land. The forty days of Elijah were a proper prelude to the solemn scenes of Horeb, and the close of his prophetic ministry. The forty days allowed to Nineveh prepared them to avert the wrath of God by repentance. The forty days of fasting and temptation in the wilderness prepared Jesus to enter on his public work as Mediator. Hence when we reach the last forty days in this long series, we are prepared to find it a period of preparation for what was to follow. Such accordingly was the fact. It was an introduction to the opening of the New Dispensation, for it was spent by Jesus in "speaking of the things pertaining to the kingdom of God." It was to Jesus himself a season of preparation for the glories of the ascension, and the return to heaven, when the everlasting doors were lifted up, to let the King of Glory in. And it was especially so to his disciples, for in the interviews accorded to them during this interval, they were fully instructed on many points concerning which they had hitherto been but imperfectly informed. And these forty days were the preparation for the wonderful scenes of Pentecost.

There are few ordinary readers of the Scriptures who are aware of the riches of this portion of our Lord's life on earth, or the number of important doctrines and principles that were brought to view during these interviews. There are few doctrines of the New Testament that do not come legitimately under the scope of this period of the life of Jesus. It furnishes to a remarkable degree an epitome of Christian doctrine and practice, even in the brief records we have of the facts. Doubtless there are many points that have not been recorded. The brevity of the record has left some things in obscurity, and created difficulties in the interpretation of this portion of our Lord's life, that every careful reader has encountered. It is in the hope of drawing attention to this wonderful and rather neglected portion of the earthly life of Jesus, and of throwing some light on the various points included in it, that this volume has been prepared. In its preparation these difficulties have not been avoided, and whilst all formal criticism and learned discussion have been omitted, as far as possible, yet the results of the most careful and laborious investigation have been embodied in the presentation of the successive subjects. There is one feature that may require some apology, as it is a departure from the usual method of treatment. It is the discarding of all attempts to make a harmony of the four records of the Apostolic commission. The difficulty of doing this has been felt by every student, and the marvel is, that we should not conclude that there was a reason for having four forms of this commission, and that it was never intended that they were to be clipped and mosaicked into one. The advantage of taking the facts as they stand, rather than trying to make a harmony of them, as is usually done, will appear in the sequel. The gospel is a harp with four strings, and the attempts to twist them all into one string really destroy the harmony, instead of creating it.

In the preparation of this work, use has been made freely of every available help, and especial obligation should be acknowledged to the writings of Grierson, Trench, Adams, J. A. Alexander, Stier, Bengel, and others, whose labours have been greatly useful in casting light on these wonderful interviews. Should Christians be led to study the life of Jesus with a new interest, to draw out the less obvious facts of his wonderful history, and to investigate the inspired writings with more care and satisfaction, the labour bestowed on the preparation of these pages, itself a delightful pleasure, will be richly rewarded.

CHAPTER 1

THE DARK HOUR BEFORE THE DAWN

The Picture—The Smitten Flock—Keeping the Sabbath—The Darkness ever before the Dawn.

> "When we in darkness walk,
>   Nor feel the heavenly flame,
> Then is the time to trust our God,
>   And rest upon his name.
> Soon shall our doubts and fears
>   Subside, at his control,
> His loving-kindness shall break through
>   The midnight of the soul."

"And there was Mary Magdalene and the other Mary, sitting over against the sepulchre."—Matt. 27.61.

These words present to us a picture as suggestive as it is beautiful. As a mere picture, it is exquisitely lovely, so vivid is the outline and so impressive the grouping it presents. In the background stands the Holy City, beginning to grow still with the quiet of the approaching Sabbath; and the mountains that stand round about Jerusalem, glowing in the light of the setting sun. As the light begins to fade away over the distant summits of the mountains of Moab, the last objects that it illumines are those in the foreground of the picture— the two weeping Marys, as they sit with bleeding hearts, gazing on the closed and silent sepulchre of Jesus. As that dark and dreary night goes down over the battlements of the guilty City, the last forms that are visible to us are those of these loving disciples, who are sitting in mute and motionless agony, looking through their tears on the grave of their crucified

Master. It is often said that woman was "last at the cross, and first at the sepulchre." It should also be remembered that she was likewise last at the sepulchre; that when Joseph, Nicodemus, and John had all returned to their homes, and when the infuriate rabble of the city might well be dreaded, even by men, that even then, as that awful night of the crucifixion came down upon the guilty city, the Marys were the last to leave the spot where the Lord lay. Hence, as a picture of woman's heroism and woman's fidelity, it is one of most exquisite and touching beauty.

But it is as suggestive as it is beautiful. The weeping Marys, gazing on the silent sepulchre, are but a striking type of the rest of the disciples on that mournful and memorable evening. The Shepherd had been smitten, and the flock was scattered. It is very difficult for us, with the light we have, to understand the feelings of the disciples at that time, or appreciate their conduct. We see so clearly that Christ ought to have suffered these things before entering into his glory, that we can hardly comprehend their bewildered and staggering state of mind at that period. They evidently did not understand either that Christ must die, or that his death was to be followed by a resurrection. These things had been announced to them, it is true, but they doubtless regarded them as symbolical, and could not think that he who had raised others from the grave must himself enter it. Hence when he was arrested, mocked, scourged, and crucified; when the heavens grew dark, and the earth quaked, and all nature gave token of some fearful utterance of wrath, they were bewildered, and unable to see why Jesus should be the subject of such manifestations. They had painful misgivings that all was lost; that he in whom they trusted had for some unknown reason failed in the hour of trial, and been forsaken of God; that all their fond dreams of the return of Israel's ancient glory were now dashed, and they left lonely and orphaned, the victims of some strange delusion or some fearful failure. They were realizing the first utterance of the prophet Isaiah, "We did esteem *him* stricken, smitten of God and afflicted," and had not yet reached the next, "He was wounded for *our* transgressions, he was bruised for *our* iniquities," and hence their souls were unutterably dark. They saw only the descending night and the unopened grave, and felt themselves in the valley and shadow of death, without the comforting rod and the supporting staff of the Shepherd.

Hence this Sabbath eve was the darkest that ever fell on the earth since the closing of the gates of Eden. He who seemed to be the hope of Israel and the world, was cruelly murdered, and God appeared to have abandoned the church and the world to their fate. The dawn of the next morning brought no relief to their darkened souls. The stillness of the Sabbath must have had a sepulchral oppressiveness to their souls, for it could only remind them of the dead Jesus. Even to an ordinary mourner there is something grating in the bright sunlight and glad skies, so mournfully in contrast with the darkness of the sorrowing heart; but to them with such a grief, having lost such a friend, under circumstances so unparalleled and appalling, the sweet light of the Sabbath must have seemed like a mockery of their gloom.

It is not unworthy of note, that in spite of the eager desire of the Marys to return to the sepulchre, "they rested the Sabbath day according to the commandment." With many the Sabbath is peculiarly the day for visiting the resting-place of the dead, and the cemeteries of our cities and villages are commonly thronged on that day by crowds of visitors, with many of whom it is to be feared affection for the dead is the least powerful motive for the excursion. It is often but part of that general disposition to take the time of the Sabbath for doing that which can be postponed during the week, and thus to save time which is money, by using time which is only holy. With many the Sabbath is the day for taking medicine, for visiting sick friends, for making up lost sleep, and for performing miscellaneous duties, that would cost more time than they are willing to give during the working days of the week. It is in touching rebuke of this effort to rob God of his time to do our own work, that we find the Marys resting on the Sabbath according to the commandment.

We have no desire to see a Jewish austerity infused into the Christian Sabbath, nor is there the least danger of such an extreme. But we have a desire to see it observed as a day of holy rest, and neither as a day which is saddled with the odds and ends of things for which men are unwilling to give the working time of the week, nor as a day in which release from the control and demands of labour gives a leisure that is used in education for hell, if it is not used for education for heaven. Between the Sabbath as a holy day, and the Sabbath as a holiday, we have no hesitation in making a choice; and were it observed more frequently as the Marys did it, "according to the commandment," men would more frequently enjoy such visions as they had, when the darkness of the sorrowing night gave way to the dawn of the blessed morning.

It will be seen that, in this time of deep gloom, the disciples were nearing the rise of a brighter light than had ever yet appeared on their path. Then, as ever since, God was bringing light out of darkness, joy out of sorrow, life out of death, pearls of the richest glory out of tears of the bitterest sorrow, and making the very facts that caused the sadness to be the means of working out the good. This is the Divine plan. It is needed in a world of sin, and ought not therefore to be regarded with surprise when it comes upon us. We shall find, as the disciples did, that the cloud is big with blessing and not with wrath, and that the darkest hour is that before the dawn.

CHAPTER 2

THE DAWN

The rising from the dead not recorded. Why?—The resurrection not witnessed by any mortal eye—The advantage to us of this arrangement—The dawn of the great morning.

> "How calm and beautiful the morn,
>   That gilds the sacred tomb,
> Where once the Crucified was borne,
>   And veiled in midnight gloom!
> Oh, weep no more the Saviour slain,
> The Lord is risen—He lives again."

> "In the end of the Sabbath as it began to dawn toward the first day of the week, . . . behold there was a great earthquake; for the angel of the Lord descended from heaven, and came and rolled back the stone from the door, and sat upon it. His countenance was like lightning, and his raiment white as snow. And for fear of him the keepers did shake and became as dead men."—Matt. 28. 1—5.

It is a remarkable fact, that the actual scene of the resurrection of our Lord, not only was not witnessed by any human eye, but is not recorded by any of the evangelists. This is a striking fact, the significance of which is commonly overlooked. Indeed the fact itself has not been noticed, and yet it is a fact of no small interest. They record the closed grave, the watch, and the seal, on the evening of the sixth day. They then record the open and empty grave on the morning of the first day, but that mysterious and stupendous event by which the grave was emptied is not recorded. It is announced immediately by the angels as having taken place, and afterwards established by the most unanswerable evidence; but its actual occurrence is not recorded by any of the sacred writers. The omission is a very remarkable one, considering the momentous importance of the occurrence itself. Had these writers been inventing a fiction, such an omission would have been incredible. This fact being the main fact of the story, it would have been narrated with details of time and attendant circumstances in the most careful manner, so that all cavil should be excluded. But inasmuch as there was really no eyewitness to the fact itself, in its actual occurrence, they refrain from recording that occurrence, with a strict and scrupulous regard to historical accuracy that is very striking; and that is one of those minute marks of absolute verity that would never occur to an inventor, but which, when brought to our notice, illustrates the conscientious and careful truthfulness of the writers in the most convincing manner.

The nearest approach to such a record is in the words of Matthew above, but this only records the opening of the grave by the angel, an event of which there were eyewitnesses in the keepers, but not the actual rising from the dead and coming forth from the grave, of which there was no eye-witness. It is obvious from the record, that the resurrection must have taken place about the dawning of the day, and was perhaps coincident with the rolling away of the stone by the angel; but this fact is matter of inference and not of record. Hence, to attempt a description of this sublime and stupendous scene, would be to attempt what the evangelists have not attempted, and to supplement the records of inspiration. A veil of deep mystery and awe is hung over the actual event, which it were presumption in us to endeavour to remove.

But the question may naturally be asked, Why was it thus left? Why were the death and the ascension made to occur in the presence of witnesses, whilst the resurrection, an event that is declared to lie at the foundation of the whole system of Christianity, was witnessed by none? Why did not Christ rise in the presence of a crowd, as he had died, and thus compel their belief in his divine mission, and their recognition of his claims as Messiah?

It might be sufficient to reply, that it is no part of the scheme of redemption to compel belief, and that we have no right to either expect or demand more than sufficient evidence to warrant belief. And there were reasons of fitness that doubtless required that this august and awful scene should take place, not in the presence of a clamorous crowd, but in the sublime solitude of that silent dawn, when the keepers were as dead men. But there is another reason usually overlooked, that has no small force. Whether it was so arranged for this special purpose, we will not affirm. But it is obvious that, by this arrangement, this fundamental fact of the Christian system, in which all have exactly the same interest, comes to all with exactly the same proof. To the first disciples, with the doubtful exception of Mary Magdalene, it was brought as it is to us, a matter of testimony supported by subsequent proof. The women were called to believe it on the testimony of the angels, the disciples on the testimony of the women, and the world on the testimony of the disciples. The women had subsequent corroboration of the testimony of the angels, the disciples of theirs, and we of the disciples; but in each case, the first demand to believe is on the same ground, the testimony of competent witnesses, and not ocular demonstration. The subsequent proofs in the case of the women and disciples include this ocular demonstration; but they were required first to believe on the testimony of competent and credible witnesses, just as we are, and not on the evidence of their own senses. Hence it is apparent that in this fundamental fact, all are placed on the same level; and the only question that can be raised is whether we possess corroborating proof of the testimony handed down to us, that ought to satisfy us, and that by the ordinary laws of human belief warrant and require an assent. This will be discussed when we reach the testimony.

We have here then the dawn of the great morning, the rising of the Sun of righteousness with healing in his wings. And like all the great facts that lie at the foundation of our hopes, it is so arranged as to be matter of faith corroborated by reason, supported by sufficient and unanswerable proof; but after all presented to us as a thing to be believed because it is true, and not because we can prove it to be true. The measure of our ability to establish the truth is not the measure of the truth itself, and hence faith is demanded of men as a duty, and not requested as a favour, and unbelief is a damning sin. When the day has dawned, the light is its own evidence to the open eye.

CHAPTER 3

THE ANGELIC ANNUNCIATION

The great morning—The early visit—The angelic annunciation.—I. *Proof of the resurrection.* The empty tomb:—The dilemma:—The evidence complete. II. *The importance of the resurrection.* It set God's seal to the Messiahship of Christ:—It declared him to be Divine:—It opened the dark valley—Its connection with justification, regeneration, holiness, and comfort to the sorrowing—The light cast on the believer's grave from the place where the Lord lay.

> "Hark! the herald angels say,
> Christ the Lord is risen to-day,
> Raise your joys and triumphs high,
> Let the glorious tidings fly."

> "And the angel answered and said unto the women, Fear not ye: for I know that ye seek Jesus, which was crucified. He is not here; for he is risen, as he said. Come, see the place where the Lord lay. And go quickly, and tell his disciples, that he is risen from the dead, and, behold, he goeth before you into Galilee; there shall ye see him; lo, I have told you."—Matt. 28. 5—7.

There is a slight apparent discrepancy in the different accounts given of the visit of the women to the sepulchre. John 20. 1, says that Mary Magdalene came "early, while it was yet dark," or more literally, "there being yet darkness," *i. e.* before all the darkness had disappeared. Mark 16. 2, states that "very early in the morning . . . they came unto the sepulchre at the rising of the sun." The discrepancy here is only apparent. The facts of the case doubtless were that although it had only begun to dawn when they left their homes in the city, yet having some distance to walk before reaching the sepulchre, and the twilight in Palestine being then but short, they did not reach the grave until sunrise. The one set of statements refers to the time of leaving home, the other to the time of arrival at the tomb, and they in no wise conflict. That these unprotected women should have ventured forth at such an hour, not knowing the perils they might encounter, and not even knowing who should roll away the great stone from the mouth of the sepulchre, was a signal illustration of the vehemence of their love to the Saviour. And in this instance, as is ever the case in the path of duty, the blessed instinct of love was wiser than the cold surmisings of logic, and the lions in the way that little faith always sees, were found to be chained or removed. They reached the grave unmolested, and found to their astonishment, the stone rolled away, and a being of unearthly splendour sitting upon it, awaiting their approach. The angel gave them the first annunciation of the fact that the Lord was risen, according to the promise.

The angelic annunciation of the resurrection contains two statements, 1., *The Proof*, 2., *The Importance of this event.*

✓ *1. The Proof of the Resurrection of Christ*—"I know that ye seek Jesus which was crucified. He is not here, for he is risen, as he said. Come, see the place where the Lord lay."

The angel states the question to the women precisely as it is presented to the world at large. He announces a fact, and then gives the only rational explanation that can be given of this fact. The fact is, that the sepulchre was empty: the explanation is, that Christ arose from the dead.

The undoubted fact is, that the sepulchre was empty on the third day. "Come, see the place where the Lord lay." How was it emptied? That the dead body was placed there on Friday evening, and the grave guarded by a watch of Roman soldiers, was undeniable, and equally so, that the body was now gone. If it had not been, the body could have been produced, and Christianity been crushed in its bud.

How then was it removed? But two explanations were ever

offered worthy of consideration. The one is that of the Pharisees, that the disciples stole it away while the guard slept.
This is incredible and absurd. The penalty for sleeping on
watch, to a Roman soldier, was death; and when the watch
was not protracted, but only for two nights, it would have
been unlikely that even one guard would sleep, but incredible
that the whole band should sleep, and that so soundly, that
the removal of the stone and carrying away of the body did
not awake them. Moreover, if asleep, they could not know
what became of the body, and could not say that it was not
risen.

But still more incredible is it, that the scattered and
affrighted disciples should make so daring and dangerous an
attempt. It was bright moonlight, when such an effort would
be peculiarly hazardous, even by the most courageous men,
and inconceivable by men so deeply discouraged and
defeated. They did not even believe that he was to rise from
the dead, much less feel that they must secure that resurrection. They had no motive for doing so, for if Christ did not
rise, he had deceived them most cruelly, in the most momentous interest of life, had decoyed them from their trades,
robbed them of their religion, and left them to the scorn and
hate of their own nation. There was no motive to induce them
to attempt to fulfil a prediction that they did not believe, and
secure an event which they did not expect. Hence, this explanation is absurd and incredible in the last degree.

The only other is that presented by the angels to the
women, by them to the disciples, and by them to us; and that
is, that he arose from the dead according to his promise. The
recording witnesses of this fact state that they saw him, heard
him, touched him, and had every possible proof that the body
before them was the same that died on the cross. At least ten
interviews with him are recorded, not by night only, but in
the broad daylight, and before at least five hundred spec-
tators. In attestation of this testimony, they suffered every

kind of loss, torture, and calumny, and even death itself. They had no motive to maintain a falsehood from this life, where its only reward was suffering; and none from the life to come, where all liars have their part in the burning lake. Hence their testimony was true, and the records of human history may be challenged to furnish a statement, thus attested, that was not true. If there be, where is it?

The fact that all the Jews did not believe this, so far from weakening its truth, rather strengthens it. Had they all believed it, that belief might have been ascribed to their credulous desire for a Messiah, that made them dupes of a story that fell in with their wishes, and that was not sifted as it would have been, had there been the cross-questioning of scepticism. The fact that so many refused to admit it proves that its evidence was examined with the utmost keenness; the fact that so many believed it on the spot, and died for that belief, shows that the evidence was unanswerable. Hence we are sure that had there been any way to disprove the resurrection of Christ, or to explain away the testimony of the hundreds who affirmed, under every kind of penalty, that they had seen him alive after his death and burial, we would have had such disproval or explanation from the men who were so anxious to give them. But as none has been given, we accept the resurrection of Christ as established by evidence so irresistible, that the laws of human action and the foundations of human history must all be destroyed, before we can suppose this evidence to be inconclusive or fallacious. Hence the fact announced by the angel is true—the Lord is risen.

2. *The Importance of the Resurrection of Christ* is intimated by the urgency with which the women are sent to declare it to the disciples; "go quickly," "lo! I have told you," and the divine title given to him by the angel, "the Lord."

The grand importance of the resurrection of Jesus is the fact that *it proves him to be the Christ, and thus the Saviour of the world.*

This is the light in which it is constantly presented in Scripture. Paul dwells upon it with reiterating energy. "If Christ be not raised, your faith is vain, ye are yet in your sins," 1 Cor. 15. 17. "The word of faith which we preach" is, "that if thou shalt confess with thy mouth the Lord Jesus, and shalt believe in thine heart that God hath raised him from the dead, thou shalt be saved." Rom. 10. 8, 9. So important was it deemed, that the apostles were ordained as an extraordinary body of men, to be witnesses of this fact; and hence it was essential to the apostolic office, that he who bore it, should have seen the risen Redeemer. Acts 1. 22; 1 Cor. 9. 1.

The reason for the fundamental position given to this fact is not obscure. Our Lord based his whole claim to be the Messiah on this issue. "Destroy this temple, and in three days I will raise it up" was the challenge to rest the whole question of his Messiahship on his resurrection from the dead. John 2. 19. Hence, if he had not risen from the dead, his claim must have been destroyed.

But there was a reason yet deeper, because of which these very challenges were made. It was the only fact that could authenticate such a claim as his, to be the Saviour of the world. He declared himself to be the great sacrifice for sin, and the Redeemer, who had opened up a passage from man the sinner, to God the Sovereign; from an earth all dark with the curse of death, to a heaven all bright with the blessing of eternal life. But how shall we know that the sacrifice is accepted, and the way open? How shall we know that he who died on the cross did not die, as all others die, for his own sin? How shall we know that he can carry us through the dark valley, and present us faultless before the throne, on the ground of his atoning work? Only by his returning from the presence of the Judge, and assuring us that the debt of sin is cancelled; by his returning from behind the veil in the Holiest of all, and assuring us that the sacrifice is accepted; by his returning from the dark valley, and assuring us that the monster is slain which made it terrible. This, Christ did in his resurrection, and hence its fundamental importance as the central fact of the Gospel.

With our instinctive dread of that dark unknown that lies beyond death, we need a Saviour who is evidently stronger than death, and who has shown his power to conquer it. We want to know that he can carry us through those awful shades, and bring us safely to the bright land beyond. We stand shivering on the shore of a vast ocean, and shrink as we gaze on its silent and illimitable waters; and we need a voice that can assure us that he who invites us to enter the ark has himself made the perilous passage, and can bring us in safety to the distant and unseen isles of the blest. Hence, it was needful that he who is to be our trust in death, should come back from that unknown sea, and assure us that he was able to carry us to those blessed abodes, where the storm and the night never come. This made it needful that Christ should return from the dead.

But the resurrection of Christ also *confirmed his claims to be a divine Saviour.*

The angels do not speak of him to the women as their Lord, but as "*the* Lord;" as the Lord of angels as well as of men, the one Lord, who can be nothing less than divine. Their reference to the place where he lay was a kind of exulting implication that he could not be held by the power of the grave, because of his supreme and divine Lordship. Hence, Paul alleges he was "declared to be the Son of God, with power, according to the spirit of holiness, by the resurrection from the dead." It is not meant that the fact of resurrection implied Divinity, for others had arisen from the dead who were not divine. Nor is it meant that the resurrection constituted Christ the Son of God, for he was that before he entered the world, the angels being called to worship him, when as the first begotten Son he was brought into the world, Heb. 1. 6. But he was "declared" to be the Son by the resurrection, since God thus endorsed his claims to that effect, during his life, by raising him from a death to which he had been condemned for making these claims. Hence, his resurrection proves him to have been "God manifest in the flesh," the divine, incarnate Word.

The resurrection of Christ also *confirms and connects the great doctrines of the Christian system.*

Many of the types and shadows of the Old Testament receive their full significance only from their connection with this great fact. The new life of Noah from the ark and the deluge, the wonderful offering and deliverance of Isaac, the living bird in the purification of the leper, the living goat on the great day of atonement, and other facts of the Old Testament—all receive their full illumination, only by connecting them with the resurrection of our Lord.

But equally does it illustrate and enforce the great doctrines of the new Testament.

Is *justification* enforced? It is by the triumphant reference to this fact, as the evidence that this justification is now complete. "It is God that justifieth, who is he that condemneth? It is Christ that died, yea, rather that is risen again—who also maketh intercession for us," Rom. 8. 33. This justifying righteousness shall be "imputed" to us, "if we believe on him that raised up Jesus our Lord from the dead; who was delivered for our offences, and raised again for our justification," Rom. 4. 24, 25.

Is *regeneration* taught? It is by linking it with this fact as its necessary antecedent, and its great type. "You hath he quickened, who were dead in trespasses and sins, . . . together with Christ, and hath raised us up together, and made us sit together in heavenly places in Christ Jesus." "What is the exceeding greatness of his power to us-ward who believe, according to the working of his mighty power, which he wrought in Christ when he raised him from the dead," Eph. 2. 1, 5; 1. 19, 20. "Buried with him in baptism," [the baptism of the Spirit, which is regeneration,] "wherein also ye are risen with him through the faith of the operation of God, who hath raised him from the dead," Col. 2. 12. The apostle argues our new life from the resurrection of Christ, in Rom. 6. 2—12, showing that as we have died with him, by our spiritual connection with his death, so we must live with him spiritually, as he rose from the dead; since the same Holy Spirit that quickened his body is granted to regenerate our souls.

Is *holiness of heart and life* enjoined? It is by appealing to the same fact. "If ye then be risen with Christ, seek those things which are above . . . Set your afffection on things above," Col. 3. 1, 2. The loftiest aspiration that the apostle could breathe for himself and others was that they might know Christ, and "the power of his resurrection," Phil. 3. 10; and the climax that he gives to a most impressive exhibition of his Christian life is, "always bearing about in the body the dying of the Lord Jesus, that the life also of Jesus might be made manifest in our body." 2 Cor. 4. 10.

Is *comfort* offered? It is rested on this great fact. To the trembling apostle in Patmos, the word of cheer that Christ himself uttered was, "Fear not! . . . I am he that liveth and was dead, and, behold, I am alive for evermore," Rev. 1. 18. To the bereaved mourner, the word of comfort to assuage sorrow is, "If we believe that Jesus died and rose again, even so them also which sleep in Jesus will God bring with him," 1 Thess. 4. 14. And when he who spake as never man spake, would give comfort to the weeping sisters of Bethany, it was with the sublime words, "I am the resurrection and the life." John 11. 25.

These words of Christ suggest another aspect of great importance in the resurrection of our Lord. *It secures and illustrates our own resurrection.*

The apostle Paul in that magnificent argument for the resurrection, contained in 1 Cor. 15, makes the resurrection of

Christ the firstfruits and guaranty of the resurrection of his people. This fact settles the questions that have been raised in regard to the nature of the resurrection body, its identity with the body that died, and kindred speculations. If the resurrection of Christ is the example, then the same body that was put into the grave shall hear the voice of the Son of God, and come forth from the grave; all apparent difficulties notwithstanding. We know not how the dead are raised or with exactly what body they come; but we know that as the same body which was laid in the grave arose from it, in Christ's case, so "He that raised up Christ from the dead, shall also quicken your mortal bodies by his Spirit that dwelleth in you," Rom. 8. 11. We can therefore safely leave all questions of this kind to be solved by the "power of God."

It will thus be seen how vitally important this great fact is in the Christian system. It lies at the very foundation of that system, and runs through all its parts. It is the great fact that assures a dying world, that there is one who has conquered death, and brought life and immortality to light in the Gospel. It is the great demonstration to a perishing race, that Christ is mighty to save, and may be trusted by every creature. It is the precious fact that has hallowed the grave, and made it but a couch of repose to the slumbering dust that shall awake on the great morning that is one day to dawn on earth; just as the body of Christ did, when the angel descended from heaven, and the earthquake shook the grave. Hence it whispers comfort to the mourner, for it tells him that the parted shall meet again, and the form that has been laid down in corruption, shall come forth in incorruption, like to Christ's glorious body. Hence, also, it disarms death of its terror to the believer, and transforms the grave into a quiet garner where the precious dust shall be safely treasured, until the trumpet shall sound, and the dead be raised incorruptible.

Thus we can easily see why the angels urged the women to go quickly and tell the glad tidings, that the Lord was risen.

CHAPTER 4

THE FIRST APPEARANCE—
LOVE WEEPING AT THE SEPULCHRE

The first appearance, why to Mary Magdalene—The order of events—The
unspoken name—The two words—"Touch me not"—The brother's message.
The two mourners: I. The spiritual mourner—The cause of spiritual gloom—
The cure—The test—Rabboni. II. The natural mourner—The bereaved—The
disappointed—The fearful—The cure of all earthly sorrow.

> "Why art thou cast down, O my soul?
> And why art thou disquieted within me?
> Hope thou in God! For I shall yet praise him,
> Who is the health of my countenance,
> And my God."
> —Psalm 42. 11

"Now when Jesus was risen early the first day of the week, he
appeared first to Mary Magdalene, out of whom he had cast seven
devils."—Mark 16. 9.

"But Mary stood without at the sepulchre weeping: and as she
wept, she stooped down and looked into the sepulchre, and seeth
two angels in white, sitting, the one at the head, and the other at
the feet, where the body of Jesus had lain. And they say unto her,
Woman, why weepest thou? She saith unto them, Because they
have taken away my Lord, and I know not where they have laid
him. And when she had thus said, she turned herself back, and saw
Jesus standing, and knew not that it was Jesus. Jesus saith unto her,
Woman, why weepest thou? whom seekest thou? She, supposing
him to be the gardener, saith unto him, Sir, if thou have borne him
hence, tell me where thou hast laid him, and I will take him away.
Jesus saith unto her, Mary. She turned herself, and saith unto him,
Rabboni: which is to say, Master. Jesus saith unto her, Touch me
not; for I am not yet ascended to my Father: but go to my brethren,
and say unto them, I ascend unto my Father and your Father, and
to my God and your God. Mary Magdalene came and told the disciples that she had seen the Lord, and that he had spoken these
things unto her."—John 20. 11—18.

The first appearance of our Lord was to Mary Magdalene. The reason for this distinguishing favour was probably because of the deeper intensity of her love. The first honour was to be placed on the first grace, that love, which is the crowning grace of the Christian life. As far as we can judge from outward expressions of affection, the love of Mary Magdalene was of a peculiar intensity. That she was an abandoned woman, as is commonly supposed, does not appear from Scripture, and is not probable. She had seven devils cast out of her; but demoniacal possession was not a state of vice, but of disease. She may have been only a diseased woman, relieved by our Lord, who had suffered much, and hence loved much. The intensity of her love is proved by her conduct.

The order of events connected with this first appearance seems to be as follows:—The women, including Mary Magdalene, came to the sepulchre and found it empty. Mary Magdalene, in the first shock of her disappointment at finding the grave empty, did not wait for any thing more, but ran back to the city to tell Peter and John, that the body of Jesus was not there. Whilst she was gone, the angels appeared to the women who were left, and delivered the message to the disciples, and they returned toward the city to deliver it. As they were thus returning, Mary Magdalene, with Peter and John, came to the grave, and the two apostles saw the empty grave and the folded grave-clothes, as described in John 20. 1—10.

They returned home, musing on these strange things, and left Mary weeping at the sepulchre. Not having waited to hear the words of the angels to the women, she knew not the fate of the body, but supposed that it had been rudely removed by the gardener, and her heart was ready to break because of this desecration of the body she so much loved. Moved with a vague, unconscious feeling of anguish, she stooped down and looked into the hollow chamber where the body had been laid, and then for the first time saw the angels, who appeared to the other women, but were invisible to Peter and John, because they were not yet prepared for such a vision. The words of the angels to her differed from those spoken to the other women, and indicate the difference in their states of mind. They were affrighted at the sight of these heavenly messengers, and hence they were addressed with the words, "Fear not," to soothe their fear. Mary, with the fearlessness of a mourning love, too intense to give room for any other feeling, was addressed with words directed not to fear but to grief, "Why weepest thou?" This simple incident lays bare the feelings of each, and shows the absorbing intensity of Mary's love to Jesus, that left no space for any feeling that referred to herself, like the emotion of fear. In reply to this question of the angels, she said, "They have taken away my Lord, and I know not where they have laid him." Hearing at this instant a step behind her, she partly turned around, and saw some one, whom, with her eyes blinded with tears, she did not recognize. He repeated the question, "Why weepest thou?" Supposing him to be the gardener, in the tearful glance she had given backward, she said, "Sir, if thou have borne him hence, tell me where thou hast laid him, and I will take him away."

Here again we see the deep love of her heart. She does not reply directly to the supposed gardener, as she had to the angels, because she suspected him of being the violator of the grave, and felt a rising of resentment at this intrusion into her grief. To the angels, whom she thought to be sympathizing friends, she tells her grief; to the supposed author of the removal of the body, she only asks to be allowed to relieve him of what he had treated as an incumbrance. And she utters no name. Perhaps she thought, in the fulness of her heart, that there was but one being that could occupy the thoughts of any one, as there was then with her but one object of solicitude. Perhaps she felt that sacredness that often hallows the name of the dead in the lips of the living, making it an unspoken word, the name of one in heaven, which to utter on earth, were a species of sacrilege. Whatever be the exact reason, it is evident that her heart was full, almost to bursting, as she uttered these words.

Then occurred a scene of most impressive beauty. But two words were spoken; but they were full of meaning. Jesus said to her, "Mary!" and at once the old, familiar tones of love announced the blessed one, whom she mourned; and turning completely round, she flung herself at his feet in a gush of rapturous embrace, and from the depths of a glad heart exclaimed, "Rabboni," "My Master! my Lord!"

She would fain have clung to his feet and indulged the luxury of gladness, but Jesus forbade her, saying, "Touch me not, for I am not yet ascended to my Father." This prohibition was very remarkable, because in a few minutes afterwards he allowed the women to do the very act here forbidden to Mary. The reason of this difference will then be more fully discussed. In this case, it was doubtless because of erroneous impressions under which Mary laboured in regard to him, and which she expressed by this forbidden act. She thought doubtless that he had returned to life, to remain with them on earth, and set up a visible kingdom, and she may have uttered words to that effect, a fact indicated by the name with which she addressed him, Rabboni. Christ desired to correct this error, and hence checked the act that was its expression. He thus assured her that the time for this anticipated enjoyment had not yet come. He was not yet entered upon that final condition where this loving intercourse could be enjoyed, and where a whole eternity would give scope for every expression of love. In the present state of transition, duty was more sacred than delight, and must ever be preferred. Hence he forbids the indulgence of those feelings of delight, and bids her go to the disciples, who were indulging the same dream of an earthly kingdom, and tell them the same corrective truth. "I ascend to my Father and your Father, to my God and your God." There is an exquisite tenderness in this message to the drooping disciples. He calls them not his disciples but his brethren, the children of a common Father and God, to assure them in their discouragement that he still loved them, and forgave their sorrowful desertion of him in his hour of need. He thus assures them that they had not forfeited his affection, or lost their brotherhood by their conduct. Such a message at such a time was full of the most unspeakable tenderness, and doubtless was so felt by the dispirited disciples, when delivered by Mary.

The whole scene is one of the most ardent love on the one side, and the most touching tenderness on the other, and is full of instruction. There were two causes of grief to Mary, and hence two cases of mourning love are illustrated: the one spiritual, the other natural. Let us look at them both.

1. *The spiritual grief.* Mary mourned an absent Saviour. She wept because the tomb was empty, and she knew not where they had laid him. There was no lack of love. Her tears proved her love. There was no lack of a certain kind of faith. She believed as far as she comprehended. Her error was that she did not know that Christ meant all that he said, when he declared that he would rise from the dead. She did not take him simply at his word, as that word was uttered, and hence she was in darkness.

Do we not often repeat the same error in our spiritual gloom? We mourn an absent Lord. Our hopes are gone; and the candle of the Lord that once shone bright, is now gone out. We may have stood at the cross, and gazed with tearful eyes at the thorns, the nails, and the spear, as we saw Christ evidently crucified before us. We may have gone to the sepulchre, and seen the place where the Lord lay. We may be convinced in a word that Christ died for sinners, and be deeply moved by the love displayed in that death, but we have no hope that he is our Saviour, and as we look into our hearts, we find no comfort, nothing but "an aching void," and we say sadly, "They have taken away my Lord, and I know not where to find him." We find in our hearts an empty sepulchre, not a risen Saviour.

Let us then go to Mary weeping at the grave, and try to comfort her. She feels that if she had loved her Saviour as she ought, she would not thus have lost him. She is forsaken because she has no part in this atoning Saviour. Would we not say to her, "Would you weep thus, O Mary, if you did not love? Would you mourn thus an absent Lord, if you had no delight in his presence? Are not your tears a proof of your love?"

The reasoning we feel would be correct in her case; and is it less correct in your case, O drooping disciple? You too are mourning an absent Saviour, and not only mourning but seeking him. You have not remained at your home in the city, but have gone forth, rising early and seeking him, where he is likely to be found. You have sought him as you went to the mercy-seat, to the Word, to the house of God, and to the Lord's table, saying, "Oh, that I knew where I might find him!" But would you thus long for him, if you had no love for him? Would you thus desire his presence, if you had no delight in him? May he not be, is he not near you, though your eyes, all blinded as they are with tears, cannot see him? Is he not even now gently saying, "Why weepest thou? whom seekest thou?"

Your error is probably the same with Mary's. There is genuine love, and genuine faith, but you are looking for an evidence on which to rest your hope, that you have no right to expect. Mary was sad, because she looked for something more than the simple assurance of Christ, that he would rise again. She did not receive Christ's words in their simplicity. She obeyed him, believed him, loved him, and sought him, but did not rest simply on his promise. And is it not so with you, O mourner? You are striving to obey, believe, love, and seek

Christ, but you are looking for something more than the simple word of his promise as the ground of your personal hope. You are looking into your dark and cold heart to find some great work there, some great voice, some great light or power within, instead of simply believing the word of promise. You are looking to see the angel descend and roll away the hard and heavy stone that rests on this flinty sepulchre, and see the dead come forth before your eyes, and hear him announce to you that Christ is formed within you the hope of glory. This is the cause of your sorrow. You have forgotten the word of promise on which you are to hope. "Look unto me, and be ye saved." "Believe, and thou *shalt* be saved." You have been seeking for something more than the word of Christ as your ground of hope, some inward working, some new revelation to you individually, which would be a virtual dishonour of the written Word, and hence you are sad. Only believe. Look away from the empty grave of your heart to Christ, and gaze and listen, and look and love, and ere you are aware, you will find yourself rejoicing in his presence and sense of his love, and your soul as the chariots of Amminadib.

If you desire a test of your heart, you have it in the words of Jesus and Mary. There were but two words spoken, but they were full of meaning. They were *names*, and as such embodied the very essential relations of the persons named. Jesus addressed her with the tender, familiar name by which she was known to him as a disciple. There was no elaborate reasoning, no new truth, only that one word of gentle expostulation and tender reproach. Mary! "Do you not know me? Do you not remember the words of my promise?" It was by simply hearing the voice of Jesus, though it uttered no new truth, that the heart of Mary leaped in responsive love, and cried, "Rabboni, my Master." Here is the test of discipleship, and faith. You may say "Immanuel, Jesus, Saviour," may love to think of Christ as the Redeemer from suffering, but do you also say "Master," and love to obey his commandments? Do you take him as your Master, your King, and try to keep all his precepts? If so, be of good comfort, for he calleth thee. If your heart is ever ready to say "Rabboni", is now saying it by a holy and willing obedience to all his commands, he is near to you though you see him not; and you have only to turn away from the empty grave, to look away from your cold and dark heart, and you shall find as you look backward and upward, that it is his voice that says to you, "Why weepest thou? whom seekest thou?" Then look to Jesus and listen to Jesus, O mourner, if you would rejoice. Look upward, not downward, outward, not inward, to the work of Jesus, his finished righteousness in heaven, and not to the work of the Spirit yet unfinished in your heart on earth; and then and thus only your tossing heart shall find rest.

2. *Natural grief* may also find some consolation from this scene at the sepulchre. Mary had lost her dearest earthly friend, and felt that she was alone, and that earth had lost a portion of its light to her weeping eyes. She was a bereaved mourner.

Here also, she can have many to sympathize with her. You also are a bereaved mourner. That sweet infantile face that once was so bright with smiles is now cold and still in the coffin, and the clods of the valley are resting on that little form that you have so often strained to your heart. Or you have seen the grave close on the silent remains of one who has walked life's pilgrimage with you for many a day, and whose removal leaves you stricken, widowed, lonely, with an unutterable desolation.

But if you are not weeping without hope, there stands near you at the grave, another form that says in reproachful tenderness, "Why weepest thou?" And if, in the anguish of an unsubdued grief, your heart would say with Mary, "Give me back my dead, tell me where you have laid him that I may come and take him away," the same reproving though gentle call comes to you. Mary! "Was it not I who took away? Did I not take the little lamb to a greener pasture and a brighter sky than any to be found below? Did I not take the partner of your earthly joys away, that you might be a partner in heavenly joys? And can you not submit to it humbly, when I have done it?" As soon as a loving heart can hear this voice, its response will be, "Rabboni!" "It is the Lord, let him do what seemeth him good." "The Lord gave and the Lord hath taken away, blessed be the name of the Lord." "Nevertheless, not my will, O God, but thine be done."

So is it with every form of earthly sorrow. To the wreck of hopes, the loss of property, the coldness of friends, all that usually darkens life, will we be rendered more submissive by this simple recognition of the sovereignty of Christ, that is implied in the word Rabboni. He is our Master, and has a right to assign to us, as his servants, what he deems best, and in the end we shall see that it was best; and the first step to that sight, is that of sweet, unmurmuring submission to the will of Christ, as our Sovereign Lord.

The same thought may be carried on to the future, so as to remove our fears. We perhaps dread the coming of unknown sorrows, more than the endurance of those that are known. We can bear those that we now have, but we shrink from what may happen in the future, sickness, disappointment, poverty, reproach, or that dark and fearful valley that lies between us and a vast eternity. These excite our dread. But if you now obey the voice of Jesus in his commands, you shall then hear the voice of Jesus in his comforts. When you pass through the rivers, he will be with you. When you walk through the fire, even though it be a furnace seven times heated, there shall be beside you a form, like unto the form of the Son of God. And when at last you begin to enter the dark valley, he will be with you there, his rod and staff shall comfort you, and his words shall not be those to Mary, "Touch me not, for I have not yet ascended to my Father and your

Father," but "Come up hither," and the weary shall be at rest.

We have then, in this scene at the sepulchre, much comfort for every mourner, who weeps with a heart that loves the Saviour. To every such weeper, there is the assurance that whatever be the cause of the sorrow, Jesus is near the soul; and it needs no new truth, no new revelation, to bring comfort, but only to recall what has been already spoken, and long known, the "words of Jesus," the sure and unfailing promises on which we may and ought to rest with an absolute and unquestioning trust. Thus believing, and looking, and listening, our weeping may endure for a night, but joy shall return in the morning.

CHAPTER 5

THE SECOND APPEARANCE—
OBEDIENCE REWARDED

Order of events: Lessons from the second appearance. I. *The mission of woman* — Why the women selected to tell the first tidings of the resurrection — They do so still — Augustine — Alfred — Hall — Halyburton — Doddridge — Wesley — Randolph — The convicted infidel — A mother's power. II. *The salutation of Jesus*—Blessings met only in the path of obedience. III. *Jesus worshipped*—Why Mary Magdalene was forbidden what was allowed to the other women — The divinity of Christ. IV. *The brotherly appellation* — The new name — The elder brother. V. *The brotherly message* — Why meet in Galilee — The great appointment — Be ye also ready.

> "Let us obey, we then shall know,
> Shall feel our sins forgiven,
> Anticipate our heaven below,
> And own that love is heaven."

"And as they went to tell his disciples, behold, Jesus met them, saying, All hail. And they came and held him by the feet and worshipped him. Then said Jesus unto them, Be not afraid: go tell my brethren that they go into Galilee, and there shall they see me."— Matt. 28. 9, 10.

This was the second appearance of our Lord, and must have been immediately after that to Mary Magdalene. The order of events seems to have been as already indicated, that as soon as Mary saw the grave to be empty, she ran back to the city to inform Peter and John, who immediately came in great haste to see the sepulchre. Meanwhile, the women, whom Mary had left, saw the vision of angels, and turned back to the city to announce the resurrection to the disciples. Immediately after their departure, Mary, Peter and John came to the grave, and after Peter and John had left it, Mary had the first sight of the risen Saviour, and was sent by him to the disciples, who were doubtless in different parts of the city. All this would occupy but a short time, if we only suppose that Peter and John were lodging in a part of the city near the sepulchre. After this interview with Mary, and whilst the women were going, by a longer road, to probably a more distant part of the city than that where Peter and John were lodging, Jesus met them, and afforded them the second appearance after the resurrection. In this appearance, there are several thoughts suggested, worthy of consideration.

1. *The mission of woman.*

It is a striking fact, that both the visions of angels, both the first annunciations of the resurrection, and both the first appearances of Christ, were made to the women. Why was this? Why not to Peter, John, Joseph, Nicodemus, or some others of the eleven? It cannot be that six facts so important should have happened without design and meaning. Why was it thus ordered? Probably for the same reason that placed three women to one man at the cross, and now places three women to one man at the communion table. The female heart has a quicker sympathy and a stronger drawing to religion than the male, and hence is found more generally in a state of greater preparedness for it. It is more confiding and pure than the male, and hence receives the glad tidings with more readiness. The hearts of men come so early and so much in contact with a sinful world, that they become more seared and hardened than those of women, and therefore less disposed to believe and obey the Saviour. It was so with the male and female disciples of Jesus. When the men forsook him and fled, and gave up all hope, and refused to believe the first announcement of the resurrection, the women clung to him, even to the end, were last at the cross, last at the sepulchre, earliest to return, and easiest to believe that Christ had risen indeed. It was doubtless in view of this fact, the greater preparedness of heart possessed by the women, that those six distinctions were granted to them, and that only their eyes were allowed to see the angels.

But as we look a little closer at this fact, we find that it was not so exceptional a fact as it appeared at first sight. It seems strange that the first tidings of the resurrection from human lips, should have been, not from the lips of the apostles, who were to be the authorized heralds of this fact, but of the women who were to be forbidden to speak in the church. It seems at first sight a singular exception to the divinely ordained plan for proclaiming the glad tidings of a finished redemption. Yet, a little reflection will show us, that it is not exceptional, but the very order of arrangement that is repeated in every generation of the world. The fact is the same that exists in the case of a vast majority of Christians ever since. We first hear the story of the cross, the sepulchre, and the throne, not from the lips of a man who stands as an ambassador for Christ; but from the lips of a woman, a pious mother, sister, or nurse, who pours into our infantile hearts this wonderful tale of love and mercy. Some, it is true, are left to an early orphanage, and some to a godless parentage; but even of these the general fact is true that the first knowledge of Jesus is learned, not from the lips of men, but from the lips of women.

This is a fact of deep moment in the divine ordering. This linking of the family with the church, this intertwining of the household of flesh with the household of faith, and this interlacing of the roots of the good olive tree with the olive plants of the vineyard, is a most precious and important fact. It thus brings the gentle heart of woman in living contact with the gentle heart of childhood, and leaves impressions of religious truth that are never effaced, and are often the means under God of leading the soul to Christ.

It is, under God, to the prayers and perseverance of Monica that the church owes Augustine. It was Judith, the stepmother of Alfred, that first moulded his heart, and prepared him to be one of England's saintliest monarchs. Bishop Joseph Hall records his indebtedness to his mother in terms that place her beside Monica. Thomas Halyburton acknowledges his great obligation to the early religious training of his mother. The mother of Philip Doddridge, the mother of the Wesleys, have come down to us linked with the piety of their illustrious children. The agency of the mothers of John Newton, Richard Cecil, and Claudius Buchanan, in the conversion of their sons is well known. Indeed Christian biography is crowded with memorials of God's seal on the patient piety of praying mothers. John Randolph declared, "I believe I should have been swept away by the flood of French infidelity, if it had not been for one thing—the remembrance of the time when my sainted mother used to make me kneel by her side, taking my little hands folded in hers, and cause me to repeat the Lord's prayer." One of our Western Missionaries states that during a revival in his field, a scoffing infidel was at length brought to his knees, and the first cry that burst from his quivering lips, was, "God of my mother, have mercy on me."

Hence we have in these first appearances a presentation of the mission of woman. She is first to utter to the opening soul the story of the cross, and utter it in tones which, though earliest heard, are latest forgotten or effaced. This story is first heard, not from the pulpit, the press, or the lips of man, but from the lips of woman, in the sweet cradle-hymns that soothe the young nursling to sleep, as the mother sings, "Hush, my babe, lie still and slumber:" in the simple songs of the nursery, when the lisping tongue of childhood is taught to say, "Jesus, tender shepherd, hear me;" in the story of that babe of Bethlehem, cradled in the manger, and that gentle and crucified man of Calvary, whose sufferings make the young lip to quiver and the eye to fill, with such deep emotion; and in those musings of heaven that fill the child's heart, as it learns that Jesus has there tenderly folded the little babe that died, and that in that bright home above the stars, there is no night, no sorrow, and no tears. These are the deep, indelible tracings of holy things on the human heart. The boy may become wayward, and the man wicked, he may learn to scoff at religion, and grow hoary in sin; but let an hour of sickness or sorrow come upon him, and the world grows dark; and then, like the vision of an angel, there will rise in his heart the image of his mother; he will remember the time when her soft hand was laid on his head, as he knelt beside her in prayer; he will remember when that hand, then thin and pale, was laid feebly but fondly in his, as, with her dying lips, she commended her boy to God, and prayed that she might meet him in heaven; and in those hours of solemn and tender memories, the hard heart will melt, and the unbidden tears will gush from the eyes of the most obdurate, at the sweet remembrance of a mother's love and a mother's piety.

The mission then of mother, wife, and sister, is one of high and solemn import, and one, the neglect of which must draw after it fearful guilt. If she tells those who ought to learn from her of Christ the wretched babble of worldliness and sin, and leads them not to the fountain that flows from the riven Rock, but the broad, deep, rushing current of worldliness, her guilt must be heavy indeed. It is a fearful crime for a Hindoo mother to bring her child, and commit him to the waters of the Ganges, and yet that unconscious babe may pass from the turbid waves of the river to the rest of heaven. But the worldly and godless mother, with a deadlier cruelty, brings her child to a stream, whose end is in the abyss that is bottomless. Hence it becomes us to remember as we see the women hastening to tell first the news of a risen Redeemer, that we have here presented to us what is woman's mission still, to be the earliest to tell to the opening soul the story of a Saviour.

2. *The Salutation of Jesus, "All hail."*

The words of salutation that we find in every language are beautiful evidences of the fact that, amidst all the ruins of the fall, there is yet remaining in the heart of man much of natural kindness. They imply in their very structure, the existence of sorrows and danger; but they also imply that there is a power that can comfort and protect, and in many cases they are really, in form, a kind of ejaculatory prayer. Never was the word of salutation more significantly uttered than when it came from the lips of Jesus. It was then, in very deed, a benediction. The Greek word used here, is well rendered by the phrase, "all-hail." Hail is a verbal form now nearly obsolete, though substantially retained in the word "hale," healthy, in a different spelling. It means literally, all health, all kinds of health, bodily and spiritual, and indicates a condition necessary as a prerequisite to any rejoicing.

But the noteworthy fact is that this benediction came to them, not when they were seeking it, but when they were only intent on their duty. They were obeying the commands of the angel, when they enjoyed the appearance of Christ.

Thus is it also with the mourning Christian. Obedience is the pathway to blessing. If a Christian is mourning an absent Lord, and has lost his hope, instead of sitting down in repining sorrow, let him go and tell his brethren some message from the Word, go and do his duty and work for Christ, and he shall find in his own experience, that it is more blessed to give than to receive, that whilst he comforts others he is himself comforted; and like the freezing traveller in the Alps, as he labours to recall life to the stiffening frame of another, it begins to flow more warmly in his own veins. In the path of duty, his obedience shall be commonly rewarded, as that of the women, by meeting Christ at some unexpected point, and hearing from his lips the gracious benediction, "All hail!" and he shall receive the blessing invoked upon the well-beloved Gaius by the loving disciple, and prosper and be in health even as his soul prospereth.

3. *Jesus worshipped.* "They came and held him by the feet, and worshipped him."

The fact that strikes us here is, that Christ permitted the women to do that now, which he forbade to Mary but a few moments before. Why was this? Not because he loved them more than her, for to her he granted the most signal mark of his favour, in first appearing to her. The reason is to be found in the difference of feeling that prompted the act. Mary embraced his feet, because she thought that Christ had returned to remain on earth, and set up an earthly kingdom, and her act expressed this conviction, and was an utterance of welcome. Hence, Jesus forbade it, and assured her that the time for this joyous reunion had not arrived. "Touch me not!" (with such views and expectations as these,) "for I am not yet ascended to my Father and your Father," have not yet reached that final home and rest, where these hopes and feelings shall be realized and may properly be expressed.

But with the women, the feeling was adoration, not gratulation; "They fell at his feet and *worshipped* him," thus recognizing him as the Divine Redeemer, the Son of God, so declared with power by the resurrection of the dead. This feeling Jesus allowed to be expressed, and thus gave the most emphatic sanction to his Divinity, by permitting an act which evinced adoration of him as God, whilst he forbade the same act, when it only expressed affection for him as man. Had he not been aware that he had a right to this worship as God, he would have rejected it with as much horror as Paul and Barnabas did at Lystra, or the angel did in the Apocalypse. But receiving the embrace of worship, whilst he forbade that of welcome, he gave the most impressive attestation to the fact that he was "God manifest in the flesh;" "the Word that was God, made flesh and dwelling among men;" the son of David, yet "God over all, blessed for ever."

4. *The brotherly appellation.* "Go, tell *my brethren.*"

The ordinary name given by Jesus to his followers was "disciples." He never applied the term "brethren" to them but once before, and there it was made necessary by the remarks to which he replied. "Whoso doeth the will of my Father, the same is my brother, and sister, and mother." Here for the first time, as a spontaneous appellation, he calls them his brethren.

The reason of this is obvious, and lays bare the touching tenderness of his heart. The disciples had forsaken him and fled, and in unbelieving despair, had given up all as lost. Hence, when they heard that he had risen from the dead, their first feeling would be that they had forfeited all claims to his regard, and been cut off from all relations to him. It was in beautiful condescension to these fears, and relief to these accusings, that he addressed them, after all this cowardice and unbelief, not as culprits or deserters, not even as disciples or friends, but with the endearing and as yet unusual name of "brethren."

It is this long-suffering tenderness of Jesus that binds our hearts to him with so much constraining power. We also have forsaken, forgotten, and disbelieved him, have lost our first love and backslidden from him. Had he treated us as we have him, we would long ago have been hopelessly rejected. But in all our wanderings, as soon as he has seen the rising of a penitent desire to return, his message to us has ever been, "Go tell *my brethren* to return, and learn how freely Jesus can forgive." That this forgiving and loving heart is even now throbbing on the throne, he gave us token in this brotherly message that he sent to the sinning disciples, at the very threshold of heaven. The long-suffering that he had at the very door of our Father's house with its many mansions, he has still, for "he is not ashamed to call them brethren," Heb. 2. 11.

5. *The brotherly message.* "Go tell my brethren that they go into Galilee, and there shall they see me."

This message was in direct reference to the promise made before, Matt. 26. 32, "After I am risen again I will go before you into Galilee." It was therefore an assurance to them, that although they had been unfaithful to him, he would not be so to them, but would keep his promise.

But why did he make his appointment in Galilee? Why not in Judea? Judea was nearer to Jerusalem, and a more highly esteemed district of the country. For these very reasons he probably chose Galilee. It was the most distant, and the least esteemed. There was many an humble heart in Galilee that longed to meet him, but could not because of disease, old age, distance, or poverty, and for the sake of such he appointed the meeting there. It was then but another token of his love. This love appeared during all his public career. He seems to have had a yearning tenderness toward the despised Galileans. His first miracle was in Cana of Galilee; his first teaching was there; his sermon on the mount was delivered in Galilee; he was transfigured there; in Capernaum of Galilee he made his home; on the sea of Galilee he walked the waves at midnight, and stilled the storm; on the shores of that sea he called the fishermen of Galilee by miracles wrought in its waters; on the mountains that look down on the sea he spent long nights in prayer; and from Galilee came those loving women who were last at the cross and first at the sepulchre. Hence it was a new token of his love.

To us he has left also an appointment, to meet him not in Galilee or Lebanon, but in "Mount Zion, the city of the living God;" and that appointment also he will keep, if we are but faithful. He "will come again and receive us to himself," in that place that is "preparing" for us, just as we are preparing for it. Let us endeavour to be ready for this meeting, when the summons comes.

CHAPTER 6

THE THIRD APPEARANCE—THE PENITENT
BACKSLIDER

The gradation—Why appear first to Peter? I. *The successive steps of the back-slider.* (1) An unsubdued will. (2) Undue self-confidence. (3) Neglect of prayer. (4) Neglect of warnings. (5) Following Christ afar off. (6) Tampering with temptation—The Avalanche. II. *The sorrows of the backslider.* The look in the palace, and the bitter weeping—The backslider's musings—The starless crown. III. *The restoration of the backslider.* The three steps—Penitence —Hope—Assurance—The two kinds of repentance.

> "What precious hours I once enjoyed,
>   How sweet their memory still!
> But they have left an aching void
>   The world can never fill.
> Return, O Holy Dove, return,
>   Sweet messenger of rest,
> I hate the sins that made thee mourn
>   And drove thee from my breast."

"He was seen of Cephas." 1 Cor. 15.5.
"The Lord is risen indeed, and hath appeared unto Simon."
Luke 24.34.

Having reached the third appearance of our Lord, we are able to note a certain gradation in the appearances, which shows that they were not accidental, but pre-arranged on a definite plan, and designed to convey definite lessons. The first appearance was to a loving disciple, the second to obedient disciples, the third, to a penitent backslider. Thus we have three of the great graces of the Christian life, in their natural order. First is love, the coronal of the whole, the grace that is greater than faith and hope; then obedience, that is better than sacrifices; then repentance, that grace of tears and trust,

where love weeps at the cross, and looks back on the sins of
the past with a sorrow all the deeper because those sins are
forgiven. Hence we have in these appearances a striking testimony of the order assigned to these graces by our Lord, in the
Christian economy.

We learn this appearance incidentally, and not by any
direct record. But it is easy to determine its order. It must
have been after the appearance to the women, and before that
on the way to Emmaus, and probably during the forenoon of
the day.

The striking fact is, that he appeared first to Peter, and not
to John or James. Why was this? Not to confer authority or
primacy among the apostles, for this is not once hinted any-
where, as to Peter, any more than as to the women. The reason is obvious. Peter was a penitent backslider, with a heart
all broken and bleeding in remorseful anguish, and he who
signalized his death on the cross by forgiving a penitent thief,
would signalize his resurrection by forgiving a penitent disciple. He thus most touchingly taught us, that the great object
of his life, death, and life again, was to purchase pardon for
the penitent, whether he was a returning prodigal, or a
repenting backslider. Here then we reach the great lesson of
this appearance, encouragement and warning to every penitent, but especially to every penitent backslider. This is
Peter's restoration as a man, not as an apostle, that being
reserved for a future occasion. In this aspect then we will consider it, and trace, in the example of Peter, *the steps, the sor-*
rows, and the restoration of the backslider.

I. The successive steps of the backslider.

It is impossible to trace the first step in the departure of
Peter. It was probably far back in his history, and perceptible
only to the omniscient eye. The angle of departure from the
path of duty is so minute, that it cannot be traced until many
steps are taken. Like the motion of the hands of a watch, each
movement is so small as to be imperceptible, but in the end it

is found to have traversed the entire circle. Thus is it usually in every case of backsliding, and thus was it probably in the case of Peter.

But there are successive steps that we can trace, by looking closely into his history.

1. *An unsubdued will.*—The essence of all true piety is the absolute submission and unison of the human will with the divine. It is the perfection of this that constitutes heaven, and it is for the attainment of this we are to pray in that comprehensive petition, "Thy will be done on earth, as it is done in heaven." The want of this submission is proof of an imperfectly sanctified heart, and this we can trace in Peter. He was not as reverently submissive to the simple word of Christ as he should have been. This was shown in two instances. The first was, when Christ announced his coming death and was rebuked by Peter, so that he was forced to say to him, "Get thee behind me, Satan, for thou savourest not the things that be of God, but those that be of men." The second was, when he refused at first to allow Christ to wash his feet, and afterwards, when compelled to yield, wanted to go beyond the wish of Christ, and have his hands and his head also washed. These instances evince a want of that absolute submission of his will to Christ's word, that is requisite to constitute true religion.

2. *Undue self-confidence.*—The same primal law of all piety, the submission of our will to God's will, generates a relinquishment of our strength for God's strength, and thus becomes humility and self-distrust. Hence, Paul declares, "when I am weak, then am I strong," thus announcing the great law of the Christian life, that confidence in our own strength is weakness, whilst such a sense of our own feebleness as leads us to cling to God, is strength. This vaunting confidence characterized Peter. "Though all men forsake thee, yet will not I," was his rash boast. He was perfectly honest in this declaration, but was resting on his own strength too

much, in making it was sinfully self-confident, and hence bereft of that protection of God that is given only to the lowly, trusting, and supplicating spirit.

3. *Neglect of prayer.* Although the common remark, that backsliding begins in the closet, is not strictly true, it is true that it always reaches the closet. It begins in the heart, but soon appears in the closet. Hence it reaches the prayer-meeting, producing first a disrelish of its services, and then a neglect of them. Thus it was with Peter. Our Lord requested him, in connection with James or John, to hold a prayer-meeting in Gethsemane, whilst he passed through his agony there, but instead of watching and praying, Peter was asleep. So will it be found with the backslider. When the disciples come together to pray, the least guilty reason of his absence will probably be that he is asleep in Gethsemane, that he has lost his relish for prayer, and forgets or neglects the appointment for its performance.

4. *Neglect of warnings, and a thoughtless rushing into temptation.* Impatience under rebuke is a sure mark of backsliding, and neglect of warning is the sure precursor of a fall. Our Lord warned Peter repeatedly of his danger, assuring him that Satan had desired to sift him as wheat, and even telling him that before the cock would crow twice he should deny him thrice. Yet in spite of these warnings, he rushed into temptation, and therefore fell into sin. Thus is it ever with the backslider.

5. *Following Christ afar off.* Peter did not wholly separate himself from Christ, nor did he wholly join himself to him. He was too much of a believer to forsake him entirely, and too much of a backslider to follow him entirely; and hence he followed him "afar off," nearer to the world than to the Lord. Thus is it also with the backslider. He cannot openly renounce Christ, nor can he openly renounce the world, but timidly follows Christ so far off, that he cannot be distinguished from the world.

6. *Tampering with temptation.* Conscious as Peter must have been of his weakness, he ought to have avoided temptation. But instead of this he deliberately dallied with danger, and first mingling with the enemies of Christ, he stood at the gate, then entered the palace, and then sat down with the servants by the fire, listening to the revilings and mockeries that were heaped on his Master, and not uttering a word in his defence. He thought that he could escape in silence. But he was recognized and challenged. He affected ignorance in reply to the maid. He was again challenged, and denied his discipleship. He was again charged with more confidence, and then, as if to sink to the lowest deep, replied in the long unused language of the fisherman, in oaths and curses, and thus reached the lowest deep of the abyss.

Such are the successive steps of the backslider. In the graphic climax of the first Psalm, he first walks in the counsel of the ungodly, then stands in the way of sinners, and at last sits in the seat of the scorner, and contentedly and boastingly takes his place with the blaspheming and the vile. The beginnings of backsliding are like the first movings of an avalanche. There is the silent dripping and wearing of long weeks, then, when the last point of resistance gives way, there is the loosing of a few stones, the rolling of a little earth, then a quivering of the whole mass, which trembles for a moment, then moves, then rushes and thunders in wild and desolating ruin into the abyss below. Thus is it with the successive stages of backsliding, as we see mournfully exemplified in the case of Peter.

2. We see also the *sorrows of the backslider* in the case of Peter.

These sorrows began with the same that must have suffused his face when he stooped to deception and cowardice, after boasting so confidently that, though all men should forsake Christ, yet would not he. But they reached their depth of poignancy, when Christ looked at him in the palace, and he went out and wept bitterly. There was in that look an impressive tenderness and power, that all the fury of the Jews, and the terror of that midnight scene of horror, could not exert on the mind of the apostle. It was as if the last drop of bitterness had been put into the cup of the suffering Saviour. He might have smitten the unhappy recreant to the earth, or uttered some reproof of stern severity, but he does neither of these. When the last vehement denial was wrung from his quivering and ashy lips, it was as if a stab had reached the heart of Jesus, and he simply turned and looked at the unhappy man; and there was in that sad and tearful look, so much of gentle pity, and yet so much of touching reproof, that it sank into the heart of the bewildered apostle, awaked him from his cowardly delusion, and caused him so to feel his base conduct that he rushed out to find some lonely spot where he might weep bitterly over his wrong. We know not what thoughts then thronged his mind; but doubtless the past came up in his memory, with all its sweet communings, its words of kindness, its deeds of love; Gennesaret, Tabor, Jerusalem, Bethany, Capernaum, Gethsemane. All the love that clustered around these scenes, came up with the anguished thought that it was this loving and faithful Saviour whom he deserted, denied, and insulted in the presence of his enemies. The future, also, with its dark uncertainties, its possible horrors, and its certain sorrows, must have also arisen to mind, mingling fear with shame, and a dreading of judgment with the gnawing of remorse. Whatever may have been his thoughts, we know that they were thoughts of unutterable sadness.

Thus is it ever with the backslider. He may be insensible for a time, whilst the delusion is upon him, but there will always come a waking. Conscience will arise, like an angry prophet, and point to both past and future, drawing from each, visions of gloom and terror. The past, with its sweet memories of holy communings, of Sabbath joys, of sacramental gladness, of closet approachings to God, of social prayer, of the great congregation, and of all the "precious hours" he once enjoyed, will come up in mournful contrast with the dark present; and from out of the midst of this picture, there will look upon him that sad, still face, that looked on Peter in the hall, uttering in its silent sorrow, a reproach more cutting than words can embody. Then rises up the future, so dark, so joyless, so threatening, a life of weariness, a death of gloom, an eternity of uncertainty so dread and terrible. And even if there be a hope of salvation, still it is a dim one, and almost joyless. "Oh! I fear," said a dying Christian, "that my crown will be a starless one!" And in spite of all efforts to comfort her, she would still mournfully murmur, "A starless crown! A starless crown!" Such were some of the sorrows that Peter probably felt, that will come at last on the backslider.

3. *The restoration of the backsliding Peter.* This restoration had at least three successive steps. The first was the look of Christ, which produced genuine penitence. The second was the message from the angels, (Mark 16.7,) sent through the women to him by name, which excited hope. The third was the actual appearance of our Lord to the penitent backslider, which raised him to the joy of an assured pardon and restored acceptance. The first and second were necessary to the third, and had they been bootless, it had doubtless been withheld.

Such is also the course of restoration in every case of backsliding. The first step is genuine penitence, a sense of the sin of wandering from God, and such a mourning over these desertions and denials as David has expressed in that consecrated song of contrition, the 51st Psalm. We must feel how bitter a thing it is thus to wander, how base a thing it is thus to desert one so true and tender to us. And this penitence will be generated only by looking to Jesus. We must turn our eyes where Peter turned his, to the face of the divine Sufferer. Thus and thus only shall we obtain that godly sorrow, that worketh a repentance that need not be repented of. Then let the backslider look to Jesus for penitence.

If this penitence is genuine, it will involve a return to the paths of obedience, and in these paths there will be found a message of hope. "Return unto me, ye backsliding children, and I will return unto you," is found only in the paths of duty, and is a message of cheer to the returning wanderer.

If the backslider returns thus to these paths of holy obedience, and continues to walk in them, "looking unto Jesus," then he may expect to have such a sight of a forgiving Saviour and a reconciled God, as shall breathe into his heart the assurance of hope. As Peter was met by Jesus, doubtless at a time and place that he looked not for him, and yet as undoubtedly in the discharge of duty, so will it be with every returning penitent. In an hour when he thinks not, the Saviour will reveal himself to him, and he will feel that his sins are forgiven, and his inheritance sure, through the blood of atonement.

Then let the backslider look *to* Jesus, as Peter, and not *from* him, as Judas. Let him remember that it is just this that makes the difference between a genuine and a spurious repentance, between the repentance of Peter, the backslider, and that of Judas, the apostate.

CHAPTER 7

THE FOURTH APPEARANCE—THE PERPLEXED DOUBTERS

The gradation. I. *The circumstances.* The sad disciples—The love of Jesus—
The sin of unbelief—The Key of the Old Testament—The burning of heart—
Christ made known in breaking of bread. II. *The lessons to the doubter.* (1)
Honest doubts in regard to the divine origin of Christianity—"It speaks to my
heart." (2) Doubts concerning doctrines. (3) Doubts in regard to personal
experience. (4) Doubts in regard to the providential dealings of God—"Abide
with us."

> "Abide with me! fast falls the eventide;
> The darkness thickens: Lord! with me abide;
> When other helpers fail, and comforts flee,
> Help of the helpless, Oh! abide with me!
>
> Swift to its close ebbs out life's little day;
> Earth's joys grow dim, its glories pass away;
> Change and decay in all around I see:
> O thou, who changest not, abide with me!
>
> Reveal thyself before my closing eyes,
> Shine through the gloom, and point me to the skies:
> Heaven's morning breaks, and earth's vain shadows flee;
> In life, in death, O Lord! abide with me."

"And the one of them, whose name was Cleopas, answering, said
unto him, Art thou only a stranger in Jerusalem, and hast not
known the things which are come to pass there in these days? And
he said unto them, What things? And they said unto him, Concerning Jesus of Nazareth, which was a prophet mighty in deed and
word before God and all the people: and how the chief priests and
our rulers delivered him to be condemned to death, and have crucified him. But we trusted that it had been he which should have
redeemed Israel: and beside all this, to-day is the third day since
these things were done. Yea, and certain women also of our company made us astonished, which were early at the sepulchre: and
when they found not his body, they came, saying, That they had

also seen a vision of angels, which said that he was alive. And certain of them which were with us went to the sepulchre, and found it even so as the women had said; but him they saw not. Then he said unto them, O fools, and slow of heart to believe all that the prophets have spoken! Ought not Christ to have suffered these things, and to enter into his glory? And beginning at Moses and all the prophets, he expounded unto them in all the scriptures the things concerning himself. And they drew nigh unto the village whither they went: and he made as though he would have gone further. But they constrained him, saying, Abide with us; for it is toward evening, and the day is far spent. And he went in to tarry with them. And it came to pass, as he sat at meat with them, he took bread, and blessed it, and brake, and gave to them. And their eyes were opened, and they knew him; and he vanished out of their sight. And they said one to another, Did not our heart burn within us, while he talked with us by the way, and while he opened to us the scriptures? And they rose up the same hour, and returned to Jerusalem, and found the eleven gathered together, and them that were with them, saying, The Lord is risen indeed, and hath appeared to Simon. And they told what things were done in the way, and how he was known of them in breaking of bread"—Luke 24.18—35.

We again see that gradation before noted in the appearances of our Lord, after his resurrection. The first, to Mary Magdalene, was a tribute to love; the second, to the women, a reward of obedience; the third, to Peter, an approval of penitence; whilst the fourth, to the troubled men of Emmaus, was a condescension to the perplexity of an honest doubter. Each one, therefore, had its special significance, and the order of the appearances is precisely the order of excellence in the states of mind thus signalized. First, stands love; second, obedience; third, penitence; and fourth, doubt, with an honest desire for light, which deserves a removal of its darkness and perplexity.

There are two points that present themselves here; first, *the circumstances of this appearance*; second, *its lessons to the doubter*.

1. *The circumstances of this appearance*.

There were two disciples of Christ, who lived at Emmaus, a small village about seven miles from Jerusalem, whose precise position is now unknown. They were present, it would seem, during the passover, the arrest, the crucifixion, and the scattering of the disciples. They knew that the body was buried on Friday evening, and guarded in its grave during the Sabbath. That Sabbath was spent in anxious doubts. They could not believe Jesus to be a deceiver, and yet they could not reconcile the overwhelming difficulties that attended the doctrine that he was the Christ. The morning of the first day of the week found them still doubting. As the day wore on, there were whisperings that Christ had risen and appeared to the women, but as they were doubtless afraid to be seen on the streets, whilst the city was so much excited, it was impossible to verify these reports, and they regarded them as mere baseless rumours. At last they concluded to return home, perplexed not less by these reports, than by the facts that had previously occurred. As they left the city, and saw its towers sink behind the hills, it was doubtless with deep dejection, as they remembered with what different feelings they had greeted those towers a few days before. But as they slowly threaded the winding path that led to their village, they naturally talked of the subject nearest their heart, and their words were words of sadness. As they thus traversed the hills, they were joined by a stranger, who saluted them with the kindly query, "What manner of communications are these that ye have one to another, as ye walk and are sad?"

Knowing as we do, who this stranger was, there is something very beautiful and impressive in this interview. Had we been left to conjecture to whom the next appearence would have been granted, we would probably have said Joseph, Nicodemus, or at least the beloved John. But not to them did he appear; not to the titled and lordly in Jerusalem; not to the eleven; not even to those who should afterwards be noted in the history of the church, for one is nameless, and of the other we know but his name. He appeared to humble and lowly men, as if to teach us the precious lesson that none were too poor or unknown to be beneath the notice of the Saviour. We know from his own words that he is ready to leave the ninety and nine, and bring back the wanderer from the flock in the wilderness, but we see it expressed as words cannot utter it, when he leaves the rich and the great, and even the loved in Jerusalem, on the very first day of his resurrection, and goes after these two unknown men, to solve their doubts and to lead them to himself.

The reply that they gave to his sympathizing question explained their sadness. "Art thou only a stranger in Jerusalem, and hast not known the things which are come to pass there in these days?" "And he said unto them, What things?" Here again we have a striking and characteristic fact. Jesus knew the cause of their sadness more deeply than they knew it themselves. Yet he required them to declare it. Thus is it still. He knows what our hearts need, long before our lips utter the words of prayer, but he would have the utterance made, for only by making that utterance is the heart opened fully to the reception of the blessing. Prayer opens the heart of man, as well as the hand of God, and that heart must be opened, or the blessing will not enter it from the opened hand.

When Christ thus drew forth their thoughts, we find the doubts that they had been cherishing. "We *trusted* that it had been he that should have delivered Israel." This is the tone of a heart that has lost its first love, and thus lost its first faith, and finds itself in the dark. There was the chilling doubt that all this hope of deliverance through Jesus was perhaps but a dream or delusion.

It was then that the indignation of Jesus flamed out in the stern rebuke, "O fools, and slow of heart to believe all that the prophets have spoken!" This sudden change of tone seems strange, until we recollect that unbelief is an insult to Jesus of the keenest character, and must so be felt. When a man doubts our word, we feel a glow of anger at the insult, and yet we sometimes wonder that doubting God's Word should be regarded by him with so much condemnation. Unbelief is simply making God a liar, and therefore is well made to be the damning sin. Hence it was that Jesus thus rebuked it, for it had in them, as it always has in others, its origin, not in swiftness of head, but in slowness of heart, not in the sharpness and intelligence of the intellect, but in the dulness and sinfulness of the affections.

But he did not confine himself to mere rebuke. He also instructed them. "Beginning at Moses and all the prophets, he expounded unto them in all the scriptures, the things concerning himself." What this wondrous exposition was, we know not; but we know the theme that called it forth, and that from Paradise in the past, to Paradise in the future, from types and shadows, sacrifices and ceremonies, prophecies in words, and prophecies in act, there came out, ray by ray, a blazing circle of proof that "Christ ought to have suffered these things, and then entered into his glory." Thus the Old Testament was made to gather into one vast and glorious picture, the centre of which was the Lamb of God, that taketh away the sin of the world. We thus reach the heart of all theology, and the soul of all true exposition, the key to all history, and the significance of all prophecy, namely, a suffering Saviour, a vicarious atonement, a Lamb slain on the altar, on the cross, and in the throne.

They at length reached Emmaus, as the day was fading away over the hills of Moab, and we see again a characteristic act of Jesus. He made as though he would go farther, for he will not be an unwelcomed guest in any heart. Had they allowed him to depart, they might have long remained in doubt. But they urged him to tarry with them, and as they made him partaker of their humble cheer, he did wondrously before their eyes. He took bread, and blessing it, as he did in the upper chamber, he brake and gave it to them, and suddenly their eyes were opened, and as has so often been true since, he was "made known to them in the breaking of bread." Having thus solved all their doubt, and filled their hearts with joy, he vanished out of their sight. They then said to each other, "How strange that we did not know this sooner! how strange that we could not see that, as our hearts burned within us, as he talked and walked with us, none other could thus kindle our hearts but Jesus!" Then unable to keep this glad news to themselves, night though it was, they arose and returned to Jerusalem, to tell the eleven that they had seen the Lord and had him made known in the breaking of bread. Such were the circumstances under which Jesus removed the perplexities of these doubters, and they have given us a test that may be applied to many other cases of doubting.

II. We therefore look at *the lessons that are taught us in regard to the doubting.*

The most important lesson that we learn is furnished by the statement of the doubters themselves in the words, "Did not our hearts burn within us, while he talked with us by the way, and while he opened to us the scriptures!" We have here a test given us that we may apply to various cases of doubting. These men felt their hearts burn within them whilst Christ talked with them, though they knew not then the significance of this glow of the soul. They afterwards discovered that this burning of the heart was the token of that holy Presence, a fact which they ought to have inferred before. Hence, if we can find this burning of heart in the doubting soul, we have at once a test by which to judge of these doubts, and a means of their removal. Let us apply the test to several classes of doubts.

1. *Honest doubts in regard to the divine origin of Christianity.* How shall such doubts be met? There are two courses, either of which may be adopted. We confront the doubter with the stupendous mass of the external evidence of Chris-

tianity. We may show him the mighty ramparts that eighteen hundred years have reared around the fountain that is unsealed beneath the cross, and show that these towers and battlements must rest on the Everlasting Rock, from which this living water flows. All this is well, but to the majority of men is impossible. A shorter and better way is to take the doubter within, and lead him to the fountain itself, thirsty, faint, and fevered with sin; and there, as he drinks of its cooling waters, and find his thirst assuaged, and his fever cooled, he will need no other evidence than this inward experience that it is, in very deed, the water of life. Then as surely as he knows that light was made for the eye, water for the appetite of thirst, and food for that of hunger, does he know that the gospel was made by God for the heart of man.

Let the honest doubter take the Bible, and with a sincere and prayerful heart peruse it. He shall find it to lay bare his heart, as it was never laid bare before. It interprets the soul's secret motives, explains its vague yearnings, reconciles its seeming contradictions, and in its teachings concerning sin, and the fall, gives a satisfactory explanation of the strange facts of the human heart. In its doctrine of redemption, through a suffering and yet divine Saviour, it meets the hopes and fears of the spirit, as nothing else can do, and exerts a power over the heart that no other book has ever exerted. This wonderful adaptation to the facts of the human soul, proves that it came from the same hand with that soul itself.

This is after all the highest kind of evidence, for it is simply God shining on his own work. It is also adapted to the humblest and poorest. When Gilbert Tennent was travelling in Virginia, he visited a very aged negro man, who had for many years been a Christian, and plied him with the usual objections to the Bible. "How do you know that the Bible is the Word of God, when you cannot read it?" The reply was as simple as it was conclusive: "I know the Bible to be God's Word, because it speaks to my heart." The reason was as cogent as it was simple. The Bible speaks to the heart as no other book does. It makes it to glow first with penitence, then with faith, then with love, and then with the ripe fruits of the Spirit, as no other book does, and as no book could do, that came not from that divine hand, which created the heart. Hence as the heart glows and burns under the words of this holy book, we may know that it is because the divine Word is thus speaking to the heart, and that therefore their doubts are all fallacious, and the Bible is of God.

2. *Doubts concerning doctrines.* These men of Emmaus were in doubt concerning the doctrine of a suffering Messiah. Such doubts have not yet ceased. Men are often in doubt in regard to the doctrines of the Trinity, the Atonement, Regeneration, and similar deep doctrines of revelation, because of certain difficulties that seem to environ them. How shall these doubts be removed? Precisely as those of the men of Emmaus. Take the Scriptures, and beginning at Moses and the prophets, listen to the voice that speaks through them; study the passages that seem to bear on these points, and let the light in upon the heart; and the heart will be found to burn as it grasps these high and glorious teachings concerning man, the great sinner, and Christ, the great Saviour. The heart that feels duly its sin and helplessness, will glow with exulting hope, at the revelation of a divine Redeemer, a Saviour who has borne our sins in his own body and suffered as our substitute; a Holy Spirit who will create within us a new heart, and an unchanging love, that will enfold us the end. Then it will be found that the Bible is infinitely more than a book of ethics, and Christianity infinitely more than a moral system. It will be seen that Christianity is a new life, the life of Christ in the soul of a believer, and the Bible the inspired record of this great salvation. On this record we are simply to rest in faith, and in doing this we shall find our hearts to burn within us, as we are brought into living connection with the warm, throbbing heart of a loving Saviour, in his word and work of grace.

3. *Doubts in regard to personal experience.* The number of Christians who are in doubt concerning the validity of their hopes is wonderfully great, especially among those whose bodily health is infirm. A test that may solve these doubts in many cases, is furnished by this scene. We do not ask whether you are sure that you have been born again, whether your hope is cloudless or your faith developed to assurance, but simply, has not your heart burned within you as you read the Bible, sat in God's house, approached the Lord's table, bowed in your closet, or met in the prayer meeting? And has not that burning of heart been of penitence and shame for sin, of fervent gratitude for the love of Christ, of deep longing for a larger measure of holiness, and of glowing zeal for the advancement of Christ's cause? Now whence this burning of heart? Who or what could have caused it? Could any presence but that of Jesus, any words but his have produced a glow like this? True, you do not see Christ as your Saviour; but if you have this holy burning of heart as you dwell on the words of Jesus, you may believe that he walks beside you, though your eyes are holden so that they cannot see him, and you may hope that ere long he will be made known to you, perhaps, "in the breaking of bread." "Who is among you that feareth the LORD, that obeyeth the voice of his servant, that walketh in darkness, and hath no light? let him trust in the name of the LORD, and stay upon his God," Isa. 50.10.

4. *Doubts in regard to the Providential dealings of God.* We often speak of mysterious providences, when affliction comes upon us, as if it were mysterious that God should do as he has promised to do, and as he has always done to his people. We walk like the bereaved men of Emmaus, and are sad. We think, why was I singled out for such sorrow? Why have others been spared such trials, whilst I have been called to endure them? Life thus becomes to us a pathway of sorrow, and we walk and are sad.

Then, could our eyes be opened, we would see beside us one

who walks unseen by eyes so dimmed with tears, and his words to us might be, O slow of heart to believe all that is written in Moses and the prophets, concerning me and concerning you? Ought not Christ's people to suffer such things and then to enter into glory? If the Captain of your salvation was made perfect through sufferings, must not you attain perfection by the same path? Thus as we begin with the suffering Abel, and come on down through the long cloud of witnesses, until we reach the "great multitude, which no man could number, of all nations and kindreds, and peoples and tongues," "who have come out of great tribulation, and washed their robes, and made them white in the blood of the Lamb," we shall feel our hearts begin to burn within us, and be ready to say, not only, "the Lord's will be done," but even, "I glory in tribulation, knowing that tribulation worketh patience, and patience, experience, and experience, hope," and that hope will not make us ashamed. Then if the day grows dark to us, and shadows of sorrow or death begin to fall, let us beseech the Master to "abide with us," and soon we shall arise and go, not to the little company in the earthly Jerusalem, but to that innumerable company that is found in the heavenly Jerusalem, where there is no night for ever.

CHAPTER 8

THE FIFTH APPEARANCE—
THE LORD'S DAY EVENING

The circumstances of this meeting—The physical properties of Christ's risen body. I. *Inauguration of the Lord's day*—The Lord's day, the Christian Sabbath—Its beautiful significance. II. *The blessings connected with the Lord's day, by the words of Jesus.* (1) Fears relieved. Why do we dread a spirit?—"Peace." (2) Faith confirmed—Evidence of the resurrection—Transubstantiation. (3) Light cast on the objects of hope—The same body that dies, rises.

The physical properties of the risen body—Recognition in heaven. (4) Errors corrected. (5) The Holy Ghost given. (6) Apostolic power. III. *Thomas absent*—Why?—What he missed—Missing at the last.

> "Thine earthly Sabbaths, Lord, we love,
> But there's a nobler rest above;
> To that our longing souls aspire,
> With ardent love, and strong desire."

"Then the same day at evening, being the first day of the week, when the doors were shut, where the disciples were assembled for fear of the Jews, came Jesus and stood in the midst, and saith unto them, Peace be unto you."—John 20.19.

"But Thomas, one of the twelve, called Didymus, was not with them when Jesus came."—John 20.24.

It is a fact worthy of notice, that of the recorded appearances of our Lord, one half of them took place on the day of his resurrection. We have seen that each appearance had its own special significance. The one before us is in some respects more significant than any of the others, for it has a more solemn and official character. It is the first appearance of our Lord to the apostles as a body, and his first formal inauguration of any of the peculiar facts of the New Testa-

ment dispensation. Its grand significance is its formal inauguration of the Lord's day, as the Christian Sabbath, by his official meeting with the disciples for worship, his bestowal of
Sabbatic blessings on that occasion, and his introduction thus
of the great facts in the new dispensation, of which the day of
holy rest was at once a type, and a channel of transmission.

This meeting is recorded by the evangelists, Mark, Luke,
and John, in terms which, though varying, are not contradic-
tory. The record of Mark is very brief, being but a single
verse. "Afterward he appeared unto the eleven as they sat at
meat, and upbraided them with their unbelief and hardness
of heart, because they believed not them which had seen him
after he was risen," Mark 16.14. Luke records it more at
length, ch. 24.36—49, and seems to include the apostolic
commission, which was given more formally afterwards on
Olivet, but which was substantially given at that time. Both
Mark and Luke have so much condensed their accounts of the
forty days, that it is impossible to refer each phrase to its
exact chronological place. Some of the words spoken on
Olivet may be combined with those spoken on the Lord's day
evening, as all the sayings of our Lord are thrown by Luke
into a continuous discourse. Hence we need not anxiously dis-
criminate between what was uttered the first day, and what
was uttered the last. The Gospel of John gives the sayings and
doings of these days with more detail than either of the
others, but gives no fact that contradicts their accounts. It
states that the substance of the apostolic commission was pro-
nounced by our Lord on that evening, though the formal
bestowal of it was on Olivet. Hence we shall notice at present
only such statements as seem to have been made on that evening, designed rather as an official inauguration of the Lord's
day, than as an official investiture of the apostles.

The disciples had met in the evening with mingled emotions. Doubt, hope, joy, and fear were struggling for the
mastery. But when Peter came and told them that Jesus had

appeared to him, all doubt was then gone as to the fact of his resurrection. Many doubts might arise as to various matters connected with it, but the fact itself was then established. Whilst they pondered Peter's statement, a hurried knocking announced Cleopas and his friend from Emmaus, who related their wonderful walk. As they listened to this narration, there suddenly appeared to their astonished eyes the form of Jesus himself, who greeted them with the words of affectionate benediction, "Peace be unto you."

A question here arises as to the manner in which Jesus entered the room, which has some importance. It is, whether he entered it supernaturally, without opening the doors, or naturally, as the disciples did. Many of the expositors allege that he entered it by opening the door, as the disciples did, and that there was nothing supernatural in the case. But the statements of the evangelists seem to favour the other opinion. It is expressly said that "the doors were closed for fear of the Jews," and of course fastened, and that in spite of this fastening, he suddenly appeared in the midst of them, implying that the doors were not opened. Luke also states that they were affrighted, supposing that they saw a spirit. Now as they already knew that he was risen from the dead, there must have been something phantom-like in his mode of entrance, which would not have been the case had he come in at the door like the disciples. The fact that the two men of Emmaus did not know him, and that when known he vanished out of their sight, shows that there was something peculiar in the mode of his existence. This is still further corroborated by the fact that he is always said to have "appeared," "to have showed himself," &c., to his disciples, as if visibility and the ordinary properties of a body were assumed by him at will, and did not belong to his body in the same way after the resurrection as before it.

We would not dogmatize on a doubtful point, but these facts seem to indicate that the resurrection-body of our Lord possessed material properties very different from its former condition, that it was naturally invisible and intangible, though material, and became visible and tangible as before, only by a positive volition. This condition of matter is not only not impossible, but is very conceivable, with the knowledge we have now of the various forms in which matter is found to exist. If our conjecture is correct, we have some light thrown on the physical nature of the resurrection-body of believers, the "spiritual body," of which Paul speaks in 1 Cor. 15.44. It will be material, and yet with properties that we have hitherto attributed to spirit, rather than matter, though erroneously; because we now know that there are forms of matter that are neither visible, tangible, nor limitable, in the ordinary sense of these terms. This question then becomes one of some interest, in view of its connection with these great problems and facts of our future life.

There are three facts that present themselves in this interview. I. *The inauguration of the Lord's day.* II. *The blessings connected with it by the words of Jesus.* III. *The absence of Thomas.*

I. The inauguration of the Lord's day.

This was the first Christian Sabbath. It is a significant fact, that one half of the recorded appearances of our Lord took place on this day, thus bestowing upon it a special honour, which this fact of its being the Christian Sabbath will tend to explain. But as the first four of these appearances were to individuals, it is in the fifth appearance that we find the special significance. The disciples were met for worship. It was their first meeting doubtless after the resurrection, and the significant fact is, that it was at that meeting that he made his first appearance to them collectively. As soon as they met for worship, he met with them, thus hallowing the day as a day of worship. He gave them on that day the evidence of his resurrection, as a great fact to be transmitted to all nations, thus ordaining the day itself as a memorial of this resurrection. He assured them of their apostolic authority, and gave them the Holy Ghost in part, thus linking the great blessings of the New Testament with this day. The facts, that the next meeting of Christ with them was on this first day of the week, that it was observed as a day of worship afterwards, that John mentions it as the day on which he was in the Spirit, as if it were the regular day of worship, and the day when the blessings of the Spirit were given, and that the primitive church adopted it with such unanimity as the day of Sabbatic privilege and duty, prove that our Lord designed this day to be the Christian Sabbath.

The Lord's day is therefore the memorial day of the resurrection of Christ. It comes to us, not merely as a memorial of the rest that was lost in the past, but also as a pledge and foretaste of the rest that has been purchased and provided in the future. It comes to us like a portion of the risen life of Jesus, to tell us of that better life that awaits those who are found in him. It bids the rush of commerce, the din of trade, and the eager chase of life to pause; it closes the doors of the shop, the manufactory, and the warehouse, and wiping the dust from the brow of the soiled artizan, it lifts from the weary frame of man and beast the burden of the primeval curse, and thus assures us that there comes a time when this curse shall be taken away entirely, and we shall enter upon the rest that remaineth for the people of God. It opens the house of God, and fills the air with the sweet melodies of Sabbath bells and Sabbath hymns; it unfolds to us from the sacred desk the glorious hopes of the future, thus letting down weekly an episode of heaven into our earthly life, fitting us for the duties of the one by the hopes of the other. It is thus a blessed fragment of the resurrection life of our Lord, designed to keep alive the memory of that great fact in the past, and the hope of those great facts in the future, with which it is connected, and comes to us, just as our Lord came to his disciples, with the sweet greeting, Peace be unto you. And it is a sad thing that, when this day is thus let down like a sheet, pure and clean from heaven, filled with angels' food, men should, in their brutal blindness, trample it under foot as an unholy thing, and make the day that lifts up the curse from our heads to fall back upon them in a heavier curse by its wicked violation.

II. *Blessings connected with the Lord's day, by the words of Jesus.*

1. *Fears relieved.* It is a striking proof of a consciousness of sin, that men always tremble before what seems to be a disembodied spirit. Were they conscious of innocence, they need not dread a messenger from the unseen world, but might rather welcome one with delight. Why is it otherwise? Why do they shiver with dread? Why do the hairs of Eliphaz's flesh rise with terror, and the knees of Belshazzar smite together, at the sight of a phantom? Is it not because the feeling of guilt suggests, anterior to the utterance of a word, that any message from the unseen world to us, must be a message of wrath? Is it not a consciousness of sin, anticipating that punishment that is felt to be deserved?

Thus it was with the disciples when they saw suddenly before them what seemed to be a spectre, so strangely and silently did it appear. They were affrighted. The words of Jesus were the words that they needed to quell their fears, "Peace be unto you." He assured them that peace was made with God, that the burden of guilt had been borne by him, that he had now returned from the eternal throne with a message of mercy and peace to their souls. Hence he linked with the Lord's day the proclamation of peace to the guilty conscience, pardon to the penitent sinner, and salvation to the uttermost for all that come to God by him. This day that the Lord hath made, therefore, still comes to us with messages of grace, and speaks peace to the guilty conscience through the blood of Christ, and thus relieves its fears.

2. *Faith confirmed.* Fear can only be removed by confirming faith. Hence, after he had assured them that they need not

fear, he gave them the grounds of this assurance by establishing their faith on a sure basis of evidence. "And he said unto them, Why are ye troubled? and why do thoughts arise in your hearts? Behold my hands and my feet, that it is I myself; handle me and see, for a spirit hath not flesh and bones, as ye see me have. And when he had thus spoken, he shewed them his hands and his feet," Luke 24.38—40. Mark states "that he upbraided them with their unbelief and hardness of heart, because they believed not them which had seen him after he was risen," Mark 16.14. Luke adds, that to confirm their faith he called for food, and ate before them a piece of broiled fish and a honey-comb, ch. 24.41—43.

Hence our Lord gave them full evidence to confirm their faith. They were to be the authorized witnesses of his resurrection, and needed ample confirmation of it themselves. This he gave them by appealing to their senses of sight, by looking; of touch, by handling, and of hearing, by his words.

It is a remarkable fact that the very evidence that Rome refuses to admit in regard to "the body and blood" of Christ, the evidence of the senses, is the precise evidence to which he appealed on this occasion, in giving them the great fundamental fact of the Christian dispensation. He thus laid a sure foundation for their own faith in that fact, of which they were to be witnesses to all nations, the fact that he was risen from the dead, and thus declared to be the Son of God and the Saviour of the world, with power, Rom. 1.4.

3. *Light cast on the objects of hope.* The great questions of this life are those that relate to the life to come. Among the most important of these is that of the resurrection of the body. Shall it rise? If so, how? Light is cast on these questions by the appearance of Christ and his challenge, "Handle me and see, for a spirit hath not flesh and bones, as ye see me have." Several facts in regard to this great doctrine are thus established.

First, that the same body which went into the grave shall

come out of it at the resurrection. In what respect it shall be the same, how far identity of particles is necessary to constitute identity of body, we know not. But as the same body that was buried arose in the case of Jesus, so will it be with all in the resurrection. Were it otherwise, it would not be a resurrection, a rising again, for this implies that what rises had been laid down. It would be a creation and not a rising again. All questions in regard to the possibility of this rising of the same body, are idle, for they are questions as to the power of Omnipotence, where confessedly there is no moral or even physical impossibility, but only certain difficulties. In the resurrection of Christ, the same body that died rose again, and so will it be with all.

Secondly, that resurrection-body shall not have the same relations to matter, space, &c., that the present body has. We have already seen that the risen body of Christ was probably in its nature invisible, capable of passing from place to place without feeling the restrictions of doors, walls, and material barriers, as other bodies do; and yet a body of flesh, blood, and bones, in a real and true sense. So we learn that the resurrection-body of the redeemed, whilst it will be material, will not be subject to the laws of matter as it is now, but like to that glorious body of Christ, that was visible or invisible at pleasure, and able to pass from place to place, and even from world to world, without effort or limitation, such as now chains us to the surface of the earth and the limits of the atmosphere.

Thirdly, that recognition will be possible in heaven. Christ appealed to the fact that they could recognize him as the same being who died on the cross. If then he could be recognized in his resurrection-body, we may infer that this recognition will be possible in other cases, and therefore that we shall know our friends in heaven.

4. *Errors corrected.* "As my Father hath sent me, even so send I you." As the word *apostle* means literally, one *sent*,

these words intimate a renewal of their apostolic office. But
they also intimate a correction of their errors in regard to the
office itself. They thought that this office, as well as the kingdom with which it was connected, was to be a temporal and
political power, with Christ as its visible head. This error he
corrects in these words: I am not to stay with you, as you suppose, but to leave you, and to send you forth as my representatives in the world, to finish the spiritual work that I have
begun, and to raise man from his degradation and sin."
Hence we have the great fact that ministers go forth in
Christ's stead, as his ambassadors, to finish the work for
which he came into the world, from the Father.

5. *The Holy Ghost given.* He breathed on them and said,
"Receive ye the Holy Ghost." The four emblems of the Spirit,
most common in Scripture, are, the dove, with its gentleness
and love; fire, with its fervour and consuming power; water,
with its purifying action; and air, the vehicle of life, the agent
that brings light to the eye, sound to the ear, fragrance to the
nostril, and vitality to the lungs, and thus is the great life-
bearer of our earth. Hence in breathing upon them, he presented the Holy Ghost under this expressive symbol, as the
source of their life and strength, and said to them in effect,
that as breath to the body, so was the Holy Ghost to the soul,
the ever needful source of all spiritual vitality. He also
declared to them that this divine Person was sent by him as
well as by the Father, was the Spirit of Christ as well as of
God, and the great blessing of the New Testament dispensation.

It is true that the Holy Ghost, in his plenary bestowal, was
not given until the day of pentecost, and could not be given
until after the ascension. Hence the words "receive ye," are to
be understood mainly in the same sense with the words, "so
send I you." The sending was really not until after pentecost,
and so also was the receiving of the Spirit. But as there was an
official right to this future sending them actually given, so

there was an official right to this future receiving, and also, we doubt not, an actual bestowal of the Holy Ghost to such an extent as to be a pledge and promise of the future bestowal.

6. *The official power.* "Whose soever sins ye remit, they are remitted unto them, and whose soever sins ye retain, they are retained." John 20.23.

This is that power to open and shut the kingdom of heaven, commonly called the power of the keys. It is not a judicial but a declarative power; not a power to acquit or condemn, as judges, but to declare, as ambassadors, the grounds of acquittal and condemnation. As connected with their extraordinary powers, it was a grant of authority to teach infallibly the grounds of pardon and condemnation, and to organize on these declared grounds a visible church. Hence it contained a grant of the powers of doctrine and discipline in the church— to the apostles as extraordinary officers, in an extraordinary sense, and to those who succeed them, as ordinary ministers, these powers in an ordinary sense. They were to remit sins as the priest cleansed the leper, not actually, but declaratively, by stating infallibly, under the inspiration of the Holy Ghost, the terms of pardon, and the terms of church fellowship. At the same time, Luke informs us, "that he opened their understanding to understand the scriptures," which is but another form of the power of doctrine, the ability to declare with authority as inspired men, the will of God for our salvation.

Such were some of the blessings linked with the Lord's day; blessings, all of which, in some form, are still connected with it, as the day of worship, the day of rest, and the day of instruction.

III. *Thomas absent.*

Why he was absent, we are not told. Perhaps he was sick, or engaged in some work of mercy; perhaps he thought this meeting for prayer useless, or uninteresting, that he could pray at home, or learn more there than he could at the meeting; perhaps he disliked night meetings; or perhaps he lived at some distance from the place of meeting; the night might have been cloudy, threatening rain, or the streets muddy and dark. Such reasons are very widely operative now, and might have been then.

But whatever the reason, the fact is not stated to his honour. The implication is that his absence was caused by his unbelief, and that thus his unbelief continued. He missed the meeting with Jesus, and the peace, faith, hope, and joy that were connected with it. He remained in darkness for another week, and doubtless in sorrow, for unbelief is but another name for unhappiness.

And is it not so still? Do not the missing disciples at the meeting for prayer often miss precious visits of Jesus? Is not the cause of absence also often the same? Is it not at last unbelief? Is it not that we do not believe in the value of these ordinances, or have no heart to attend them?

Let us then beware of such a record about us in the books, as we have here about Thomas, that "he was not with them when Jesus came." Let us be with the friends of Jesus now, in work and in worship, lest when he comes again, in that last, great day of his coming, the world's great evening and end, it may also be recorded of us, that when he gathers his saints together there, we are not with them, but cast out into the outer darkness. Let Jesus, when he visits his people met for prayer, find us among them.

CHAPTER 9

THE SIXTH APPEARANCE—THE SCEPTICAL DISCIPLE

The second Lord's day—The dark disciple. I. *The causes of the scepticism of Thomas.* (1) The original structure of his nature—Living in the shadow—(2) A wrong standard of belief.—The credulity of unbelief—(3) Absence from the meeting of the disciples—God honours his appointed means. II. *The consequence of his unbelief.* Wretchedness of soul—The sceptic wretched whether right or wrong. III. *The removal of his scepticism.* (1) The awakening of his faith by a sight of Christ—(2) The confession of his faith—Did he blaspheme? —(3) The personal character of his faith—(4) The benediction of Jesus— Goethe.

> I heard the voice of Jesus say,
>   'Come unto me and rest;
> Lay down, thou weary one, lay down
>   Thy head upon my breast.'
>
> I came to Jesus as I was,
>   Weary, and worn, and sad,
> I found in him a resting place,
>   And he has made me glad.

"And after eight days, again his disciples were within and Thomas with them; then came Jesus, the doors being shut, and stood in the midst, and said, Peace be unto you. Then saith he to Thomas, Reach hither thy finger, and behold my hands, and reach hither thy hand, and thrust it into my side; and be not faithless but believing. And Thomas answered and said unto him, My Lord and my God. Jesus saith unto him, Thomas, because thou hast seen me, thou hast believed: blessed are they that have not seen, and yet have believed." John 20.26-29.

This meeting was a second observance of the Christian Sabbath. It was the evening of the Lord's day, *i.e.* after the eighth day, the day after the Sabbath, which was the seventh day; and as the day, by our mode of reckoning, ended at sunset, the evening of the first day of the week was really after the eighth day had ended, and hence the phrase, "an eight days," for a week, naturally took its rise. There seems to have been no appearance of our Lord during the intervening week. Where he was, and what his employments, we need not conjecture, though this silence suggests a corroboration of the views formerly presented in regard to the physical properties of his risen body.

It would seem that Thomas, in the hasty conclusion to which he plunged after the crucifixion, that all was lost, had retired to some retreat, from which he did not emerge until after the first Lord's day. When he heard an account of its events, he rejected the whole thing as incredible. He assured the disciples that they had been cheated by an optical illusion. Had they tested the reality of Christ's body by the sense of touch, they would have discovered their error. As for himself, he will not believe, unless he has this evidence, unless he can touch the marks made by the crucifixion, and thus prove, beyond contradiction, that it is the identical body that was crucified. This scepticism might have been removed during any other day of the week, but it was not done until the Lord's day, doubtless in order again to put honour and authority upon the Christian Sabbath. That hallowed day was again to be distinguished by the cure of a sceptical disciple, in the establishment of the great fundamental fact of Christianity, the resurrection of Jesus. Hence we reach the special significance of this appearance, and the reason why it was postponed for a week, so as to fall on the Lord's day evening, the only time of the day when the disciples could meet in safety for worship. We have here then, 1. *The causes of the scepticism of Thomas. 2. Its consequences. 3. Its removal.*

1. *The causes of the scepticism of Thomas.*

(1) *The original structure of his nature.* Thomas seems to have been, naturally, a man of gloomy and saturnine spirit, prone to look on the dark side of everything, and live in the

shade. There was little in him of the bright, sunny, and hopeful, and hence he was not so ready to believe good news as bad.

This frigidity of temperament made him sceptical, and by a singular phenomenon of mind, though slow in coming to favourable, he was hasty in coming to unfavourable conclusions. This is illustrated in the only other intimation we have of him in the gospel. When our Lord stated (John 11.15) that he intended to go into Judea, on the death of Lazarus, in spite of the remonstrances of the disciples as to the peril of the journey, Thomas seems to have given up in despair, and supposed that Christ was going to certain death; but believing that there was nothing worth living for after that, he said, "Let us also go, that we may die with him." Here was a kind of heroism, but it was the heroism of distrust and despair. He ought to have known that Christ was able to defend himself if need be, but he at once dropped into despair, when he found that Jesus would do what he thought a rash venturing upon certain death.

He lays bare here the secret defect of his character. It was the want of a warm, confiding spirit. It was not clearness of head so much as coldness of heart. All scepticism indeed is a disease of the heart. It is a want of that confiding trust in truth, that is not so much an intellectual as a moral quality, and arises not so much from perception of evidence, as from sympathy with the truth itself.

This state of heart of course produces its legitimate results in the intellect, and prevents it reaching conclusions from which the emotional nature recoils with aversion.

But whilst this was true of Thomas by nature, it was also true that grace had done much to warm and open his heart. Had this natural temperament been connected with corrupt morals, he would have been like Judas, Ananias, or Demas; or later still, like Julian the apostate, Paine, or Voltaire. There never was a reviling sceptic, who was not, openly or secretly, corrupt in his morals. It was otherwise with Thomas. He was pure in his morals, the subject of divine grace, and though his native coldness of temper made him sceptical, the grace that was in him induced Jesus to take the trouble to cure, once for all, doubtless, this scepticism, and bring his heart forth to dwell in the sunshine.

(2) *A wrong standard of belief.* "Except I shall see in his hands the print of the nails, and put my finger into the print of the nails, and thrust my hand into his side, I will not believe." This was an unfair demand, and set up a wrong standard of belief. He had the testimony of ten men, who had seen and heard Jesus, and this testimony ought to have been believed. To ask more evidence, was unreasonable, and to be satisfied only by his own senses, and only that of touch, was folly. If ten men could be deceived, could not one? If their senses were imposed upon, might not his? If Jesus or any other agent could deceive the senses of sight or hearing, might he not that of touch? Hence to reject this evidence and demand that of his own touch alone, was absurd. It was, as a German writer quaintly observes, to trust his ten fingers more than the testimony of the ten other apostles.

Yet it is well that it was so, for we are thus assured that the evidence was well sifted. The fact that the ten were incredulous in regard to the statement of the women, and that Thomas was equally so as to theirs, proves that the evidence must have been irresistible, and gives us an ample guaranty that this fundamental fact must have been fully and thoroughly tested, before it was believed and proclaimed to the world.

But still it is not the less true, that all scepticism is unreasonable in its rationalism, and credulous in its unbelief. It demands an evidence for which it has no right, and in doing so betrays its weakness. Men who cannot believe Moses and Paul, believe Voltaire and Paine, Andrew Jackson Davis and the spirit-rappers. They cannot believe that the Holy Spirit has spoken to us through prophets and apostles, and yet they believe that these prophets and apostles may be summoned to rap out blundering guesses at the number of a man's children, or the age of his grandmother, for a specified admittance fee to the medium. They would deem it inanity to believe the record made in regard to the tomb of Jesus, and deride the man who would believe all that he read on an American tombstone, whilst they swallow with the utmost simplicity the mendacious legends of the tombs of Egypt. All this arises from the fact, that, like Thomas, they have adopted a wrong standard of belief. They make their own notions or senses the rule, instead of some tried and sure standard. They will not believe a doctrine clearly set forth in the Bible, because it seems to them unreasonable, forgetting that this may be as much because of the error in their vision, as because of any error in the doctrine. Hence the true course is to ascertain, first, on such evidence as we admit in other cases, whether the Bible is God's Word, and then with docile submission believe whatever is taught us in that Bible as truth.

(3) Another cause of the scepticism of Thomas was his *absence from the meeting of the disciples.*

Had he been with them in that assemblage for prayer, he would have had every doubt removed, and been a rejoicing believer. The same cause still operates in producing or continuing scepticism. It is usually connected with a neglect of the means of grace. The sceptic is not found in the place of prayer, a devout worshipper, and hence fails to receive a blessing from God. It is true that he may read at home more able discourses than he can hear at church; may be more logical and learned than the preacher; may read the Bible at home as well as hear it at the house of God; but the simple fact is, that God has not promised to bless the one, and he has promised to bless the other, and without that blessing there can be no true faith. It is by the "foolishness of preaching" that he will save them that believe. Thomas might have argued that he could worship at home as well as in the upper room with the ten, and be as much benefited; but the truth was that Jesus met with the ten, and not with him, and so will it ever be. God will honour his ordinances because he has promised to do so, and the neglect of them will commonly confirm a state of unbelief. The Saviour may be in the meeting for worship, may speak peace to the doubting, and often does, but the absent sceptic will not receive the blessing, because he is not in the place where it is to be given.

2. *The consequences of the scepticism of Thomas.*

We need present but one of these consequences, *an aimless wretchedness of soul.* In any event, whether right or wrong, he was unhappy. If right in his unbelief, Jesus was an impostor, his hopes all vanished into air, and he left desponding and wretched, a dupe of his former belief. If wrong, he had put from him the most blessed hopes that ever brightened on his path, had refused to believe the words of Jesus, and was a dupe to his present unbelief. In either case his life was an aimless and joyless thing.

The same thing is true of every sceptic. Whether right or wrong, he must be wretched just so far as he allows himself to think at all. If he is happy, it is because he does not, or dares not think. If he is right, and it is uncertain whether there is a revelation from God, a hereafter, a personal God, he cannot be happy, for he is a poor blind insect groping in the dark. He suffers now, and knows not that he will not hereafter, or that he will have any compensation for the toils and sorrows of the present. He knows not that he will ever see the face of his loved dead, or meet the lost of earth in the bliss of heaven. Can he then be happy? Have not most of the great sceptics confessed at times the secret sorrows that gnawed within? Have they not confessed the shadows that chilled their hearts, and longed for light? Hence if they are right, it is a truth that we need not care to know, for its effect would only be to make us wretched without making us better. It would only be to take away the only light that gilds the vale of tears, the only comfort that often cheers the home of poverty and pain, the only staff that supports the feebleness of age, and the only brightness that rests on the grave. It would be to take away a hope that makes men better, and give them nothing in its place but a dreary despair. If the sceptic is right, the Christian will be as happy in the future as he will be, and will either never discover that he has been deluded, or discover that the delusion has never done him any harm. But if the sceptic is wrong, he is *lost!* lost for ever! How fearful the difference! How appalling, then, the consequences of that unbelief! In either case, the consequence of scepticism is wretchedness in this life; in one case, it is wretchedness in the life to come. Can that which thus darkens in every case, and may destroy in one case, be the truth? Must it not be from beneath and not from above?

3. *The removal of the scepticism of Thomas*

In this removal there are several stages that may be noted.

(1) *The awaking of his faith.* His faith was awakened by the sight of Jesus. The Lord showed him his hands and his feet, and he saw in the ragged print of the nails the proof that he was the crucified Saviour, and that the same love that had led him to the cross, now led him to win back his erring disciple. Doubtless the unbelieving Thomas expected that Jesus would meet him with language of stern rebuke, for he felt that he deserved it. But instead of this merited reproof, it was with tones and words of tenderness that he even stooped to meet his unreasonable demand, and asked him to come and put his finger into the print of the nails, and his hand into the gash of the spear, and be not faithless but believing. There was a sublime tenderness in thus stooping to meet the very unreasonableness of his unbelief that overwhelmed the heart of Thomas at once, and swept away his scepticism in its flood of love.

Thus must faith be awakened now in the heart of the sceptic. Love is mightier than logic, because unbelief is not so much a disease of the head, as of the heart. If a sceptic is honest, and capable of discerning the truth, let that truth be spoken in love; let him be led to where he shall see "one hanging on a tree, in agony and blood," and this sight will do more to awake his faith than a thousand arguments. "I am deeply concerned for your salvation," said a pious man to a hardened sceptic, who had long foiled every effort to convince him of the truth of Christianity by argument. The words were simple, but they were spoken with a swimming eye and a quivering lip, for the good man had spent much time the previous night in prayer for the unbeliever. These words were the means of melting that proud and hard heart, and leading it to be concerned for its own salvation, a concern that never ceased until he found peace in believing. Living faith is a plant that needs not only the light of logic, but also the warmth of love, to enable it to grow, and bring forth fruit; for with the heart man believeth unto righteousness, and the belief of the gospel is not merely the cold assent of the mind to a proposition, but the warm trust of the heart in a promise.

(2) *The confession of his faith.* As soon as Thomas saw Jesus, his scepticism vanished in a moment. He forgot his former demand for unreasonable evidence, for he found that he did not need it. He was satisfied and more than satisfied, and cried out in the fulness of his faith, "My Lord, and my God!"

It is a striking proof that Thomas has his successors, to find the meaning of these plain words doubted. They so plainly call Christ God, and he so plainly receives the divine title, that there seems to be no escape from a conclusion thus asserted by the one and admitted by the other, that Jesus Christ was truly God. This conclusion is strengthened by the effort made to evade it. The only explanation offered is, that this was an exclamation of surprise, and that Thomas in his sudden amazement exclaimed, "My Lord, and my God!" But aside from the fact that a compound exclamation of surprise, connected by the conjunction "and," would have been almost absurd, and completely at variance with that ejaculatory and abrupt form that characterizes such utterances, it would in that case have been profanity. It would have been taking God's name in vain, and Jesus, who rebuked unbelief, would never have allowed profanity to pass unreproved. Moreover, it is said expressly in v. 28, that it was an expression addressed to Jesus, and not an exclamation of surprise. "And Thomas answered and said unto him, (*i.e.* Jesus,) My Lord, and my God." Hence it is a most striking proof-text of the divinity of Jesus Christ.

(3) *The personal character of his faith.* Luther says that the beauty of the Bible lies in its pronouns. It is not that we can say that there is a God, but that we can say, "This God is *our* God, for ever and ever." So it was with Thomas. Not content with saying as Nathanael did, "Thou art the Son of God," he clasps him now with all the tenderness of a living faith, and cries out, "*My* Lord, and *my* God." Tradition relates that from that hour the restored penitent never swerved in his career, but toiled in Asia, preaching to Medes, Persians, Hyrcanians. Bactrians, and Ethiopians, until at last he laid down his life for Jesus on the distant plains of India. It was a noble atonement for the unbelief of a week.

Thus must it be with the sceptic. He must be led to the cross, must see Jesus, as *his* Saviour, must be enabled to cry out, *My* Lord and *my* God, and *my* Redeemer, or he is not beyond all danger of falling back into unbelief. A personal appropriating faith, that trusts the soul to Jesus as Lord, and clings to him as Saviour, is the only certain and radical cure for unbelief.

(4) *The benediction of Jesus.* "Blessed are they that have not seen, and yet have believed."

There are many who, like Thomas, are longing for some sensible assurance of the love of Christ, beyond the general declarations of the Bible. They want some inward token that they are born again, some sensible assurance of their acceptance, before they believe and commit their souls wholly to Jesus. They desire to be Christians, but want to know that they have been converted before they trust. This is precisely the error of Thomas. They want the evidence of sense, rather than of faith. They want some inward work in the heart, as a ground of faith, rather than the outward work of Christ, offered in the gospel. Such an assurance will not be given them. Their warrant to believe is in the Word, and to give them any other warrant would be to dishonour that, and to thrust their hands into the Saviour's side before believing. They must go to Jesus, just as they are, cast themselves on his mercy, and believe that he will do as he has promised, pardon, purify, and save, and then the benediction shall descend upon them, "Blessed are they that have not seen and yet have believed." They will soon need no other evidence that they have been born again, than the conscious operation of the new life that works within them. They will not so much inquire whether they are spiritually alive, as they will not think of doubting it. In the gradual unfolding of every filial affection, and the instinctive exercise of every filial feeling, the Spirit will witness with their spirits that they are the sons of God.

We have then in this scene with Thomas the cause and cure of scepticism. Its cause is a cold and unbelieving heart, a heart that cannot warmly confide in what deserves its confidence. Under the influence of such a heart, a wrong standard of belief is set up, and the comforts of the gospel are rejected. The cure for it is to come as a little child, and obey and trust Jesus Christ, and thus make experiment of his word, as the balm of Gilead, the cure for the sin-sick soul. Goethe felt this dark longing of unbelief as he neared the close of life, and in one of his seasons of restless longing wrote a verse that may thus be translated:—

"Fairest among heaven's daughters,
Thou who stillest pain and woe,
Pourest thy refreshing waters
On the thirsty here below;
Whither tends this restless striving?
Faint and tired, I long for rest;
Heaven-born peace!
Come, and dwell within my breast."

These words, written in pencil, on coarse paper, chanced to come into the possession of a lady who understood the case. She, with exquisite propriety, wrote on the other side of the paper: "Peace I leave with you; my peace I give unto you; not as the world giveth give I unto you. Let not your heart be troubled, neither let it be afraid."—JESUS CHRIST. But the monarch of German literature was too proud to stoop to the yoke of the lowly Nazarene; and his yearnings, we have reason to fear, were ever unsatisfied.

CHAPTER 10

THE SEVENTH APPEARANCE—THE SHORE OF GALILEE

How the third meeting. I. *The circumstances.* The fishing party—The night of unsuccessful toil—The morning vision—The fire on the shore, and the food. II. *The meaning of this scene.* The picnic interpretation—Connection with the first miraculous draught of fishes—The meaning of the first miracle —"Toiling all night and taking nothing"—The inefficiency of the pulpit— The differences of the miracles, and their meaning—The second miracle shadows the final glory of the church—The repast on the shore, its meaning —Lessons to the church, now on the sea—Comfort to the individual Christian.

> "I heard the voice of Jesus say,
> 'I am this dark world's light;
> Look unto me, thy morn shall rise,
> And all thy day be bright.'
> I looked to Jesus, and I found
> In him my star, my sun;
> And in this light of life I'll walk,
> Till travelling days are done.
>
> I heard the voice of Jesus say,
> 'Fear not the vanquished grave;
> My arm, within its gloomy shades,
> Is mighty still to save.'
> I clung to Jesus, and I now
> Shrink not from death's dark vale;
> For he will walk beside me there
> When heart and flesh shall fail."

"After these things Jesus shewed himself again to the disciples at the sea of Tiberias; and on this wise shewed he himself. There were together Simon Peter and Thomas called Didymus, and Nathanael of Cana in Galilee, and the sons of Zebedee, and two other of his disciples. Simon Peter saith unto them, I go a fishing. They say unto him, We also go with thee. They went forth, and entered into a ship immediately; and that night they caught nothing. But when the morning was now come, Jesus stood on the shore; but the disciples knew not that it was Jesus. Then Jesus saith unto them, Children, have ye any meat? They answered him, No. And he said unto them, Cast the net on the right side of the ship, and ye shall find. They cast therefore, and now they were not able to draw it for the multitude of fishes. Therefore that disciple whom Jesus loved saith unto Peter, It is the Lord. Now when Simon Peter heard that it was the Lord, he girt his fisher's coat unto him, (for he was naked,) and did cast himself into the sea. And the other disciples came in a little ship, (for they were not far from land, but as it were two hundred cubits,) dragging the net with fishes. As soon then as they were come to land, they saw a fire of coals there, and fish laid thereon, and bread. Jesus saith unto them, Bring of the fish which ye have now caught. Simon Peter went up, and drew the net to land full of great fishes, a hundred and fifty and three: and for all there were so many, yet was not the net broken. Jesus saith unto them, Come and dine. And none of the disciples durst ask him, Who art thou? knowing that it was the Lord. Jesus then cometh, and taketh bread, and giveth them, and fish likewise. This is now the third time that Jesus shewed himself to his disciples, after that he was risen from the dead." John 21.1—14.

There seems to be a discrepancy between the statement of John that this was the third appearance of our Lord to his disciples, and the facts as recorded by the other evangelists. But the discrepancy is only apparent. It was really the seventh appearance, but only the third to the assembled disciples. The rest were to individuals, and were purely personal in their design. This was to a collective body of the disciples, and was of a more formal and official character than the four personal interviews, and hence was literally, as John states, the third meeting with the *disciples*. This meeting was a very remarkable one, so much so as to require its record in a kind of postscript to the Gospel of John, and is worthy of our careful study. The natural order of consideration will be, first, *the circumstances of the meeting*, and then *their meaning*.

1. *The circumstances of this meeting on the shore.*

The disciples had parted with Jesus in Jerusalem during the second week after the resurrection, and had gone to Galilee to await the great meeting promised there. Whilst waiting for it, it was needful for them to subsist, and being poor, they naturally reverted to their former employment to support them until the will of Christ was more fully made known. Where Jesus was during this interval, we know not. As already remarked, his existence during these forty days was under peculiar physical conditions, as is intimated by the statement that, when he appeared, he is said to have "shewed himself," as if he was naturally invisible, and became visible only by an act of the will.

There were at least seven of the disciples together: Peter; Thomas, no longer the doubter, and no longer absent when Jesus appears; Nathanael of Cana, who was probably the apostle called Bartholomew; James and John, who with Peter were the witnesses to so many of the miracles; and two other disciples, who, from their previous associations with the others, were probably Philip and Andrew. Peter, with his wonted forwardness, proposes that they should go and fish, to which the rest consent, but toil all night and take nothing.

If we could know the conversation of that long and toiling night, it would doubtless furnish us much that was very interesting. Peter would probably tell of his fall, his penitence, and the words of love that the Master spake as he gently restored him to his former hope. Thomas could speak of his scepticism and his restored faith, and the fervent resolve with which he now clung to his Lord and his God. Nathanael could relate his wonderful interview with the Lord in an adjacent city, and how he had seen heaven open and the angels ascending and descending on the Son of Man.

James, Philip, and Andrew, could each bring forward some well remembered fact or word, that had fastened on their memories, whilst John, the beloved, might muse in silence as he looked out on the stars and the sea, and thought of that wonderful love that was then beginning to unfold to his vision, wider than the cope of heaven, and deeper than the waters of the sea of Galilee.

As the night wore away, and the grey morning began to dawn on the wild hills that stand around Gennesaret, they turned to the shore with feelings of disappointment. As they neared it, they saw, in the dim twilight that was flushing the sky, the form of a man on the shore. There was something strange and almost suspicious in the sight, and hence, though he addressed them in terms not only courteous, but kind, "Children, have ye any meat?" they answered somewhat roughly, "No." He then bade them to cast on the right side of the ship, which when they did, they found the net so full that they could not draw it into the ship. This sudden and miraculous draught reminded the thoughtful John of another in the same sea, on a former occasion, and he whispered to Peter, "It is the Lord." When Peter heard this, he could not wait for the slow movement of the ship, although it was only about one hundred yards from the shore, and he girt his outer garment upon him, that he might present himself with decent propriety before his Lord, and leaping into the water, he waded ashore, and cast himself, doubtless in fervent adoration, at the feet of Jesus. Meanwhile the disciples left the larger vessel, launched a boat, and drew the net to shore. When they came near, Peter met them and aided them to land it, and on counting the fish, they found that they had one hundred and fifty-three, and yet their net was not broken.

As they drew near the shore a strange sight met their gaze. They saw a fire on the shore, with fish and bread cooking as if for a meal. When they had counted the fish, Jesus invited them to breakfast. There was in all this something so strange, startling, and almost spectral, that they were filled with awe. Whence and why this fire on the lonely shore? Whence the fish and bread, and yet some of their own fish to be added? What did all this mean? They desired to ask, but were deterred by that feeling of awe that they could not repress in the mysterious presence of Jesus. But at his invitation they sat down beside the cheerful fire, and made their morning repast, we doubt not, in gladness and gratitude.

Such were the circumstances of this remarkable meeting on the shore of Galilee.

2. *What was the meaning of this scene?*

There is one school of interpretation which alleges that our Lord kindled this fire on the shore, and prepared this meal, merely as an act of kindness to his disciples. He knew they had been fishing all night, and would be cold and hungry, and hence provided fire and food for their refreshment. All this is true, but to say that this is the whole meaning of the scene, is to be guilty of a most shallow evasion. Why the double supply of fish to the coals? Why were those from the sea brought, and added to those on the shore, in making the meal? Why did they delay to count the fish before they were asked to breakfast? Why is the number so carefully recorded? All these things prove that there was a deeper meaning in the transaction than the mere supply of the cold and hunger of these disciples.

What then was the design of it? The mind reverts instantaneously to another draught of fishes made in the same sea, about three years before, when four of the seven disciples here present were called. That miraculous draught was made at the opening of Christ's work, and is generally agreed to have symbolized truths pertaining to the opening; this therefore at the close of that work, or rather at the opening of a new portion of his work, would seem in like manner to embody truths suitable for that period. If the one was a symbolical lesson, so also was the other, and hence the reason for its minute record. In the first miracle, our Lord gave the clue to its meaning in the declaration to Peter and the others that they should be fishers of men, Luke 5.10. It was a lesson to the disciples as the preachers of the gospel, and a lesson that sunk deep into their hearts. The adoption of the fish as an anagrammatic symbol of Jesus Christ, and its frequent appearance in the early Christian art and literature, shows how deeply this lesson was engraved on the heart of the church.* An important lesson was taught Peter, as he was called the first time to the apostolic office, and another lesson equally important was taught him, as he was to be reinvested with it, after his fall.

The lesson taught in the first miraculous draught of fishes was the same that was taught in the parable of the net, in Matt. 13.47,48. "The kingdom of God is like a net that was cast into the sea, and gathered of every kind, which when it was full, they drew to shore, and sat down and gathered the good into vessels, but cast the bad away." In the miracle it is added that the net brake because of the number of fishes, and the exact number is not given. The lesson thus embodied is a most obvious one, and one that the whole history of the church confirms. It predicts that in the casting of this gospel net, many shall be enclosed in it who are not good; and that there shall be rents and schisms in its external bonds, of a most serious character. And has it not been so? Has not the visible church included both bad and good, both wise and foolish? And has not its outward form been torn again and again by schism, heresy,and error? And are not those who have once been brought in often breaking through its trammels and plunging again into the miry sea? It is obvious then that this first miraculous draught of fishes presented precisely the lesson that the disciples needed in beginning their work, and that the truths thus symbolized both by parable and by miracle have been verified by the history of the church.

It is most natural then for us to infer that similar lessons

*The Greek word ICHTHUS, fish, contains the first letters of the phrase IESOUS CHRISTOS THEON UIOS SOTER *Jesus Christ, Son of God, the Saviour*, and is found engraven on the tombs of the early Christians in the catacombs of Rome.

were designed to be taught by the second miracle of this kind. In both cases, they had toiled all night and caught nothing; in both cases, at the command of Christ, and by his miraculous power, their labours were crowned with success. How painfully this common fact foreshadows the labours of ministers often needs no proof. It is sadly true of them but too frequently, that they toil all night and take nothing. They go forth, wakeful and weeping, and strive to win souls to Christ, and yet are compelled to return with the mournful plaint, "Who hath believed our report?" This want of success is sometimes referred to the inefficiency of the pulpit, and we are told that if preachers would copy the manner of the politician and the lawyer, they would be more successful. This is like the assurance that with a different twine to the net, or a different throw in handling it, the disciples would have enclosed the fish. But the fact remains, that this very want of success was long ago predicted in the unsuccessful toil of the disciples on the sea of Galilee during that weary night, when they toiled, and yet took nothing. This fact that was common to both miracles, and the further fact that only at the command of Jesus their labours were crowned with success, indicate that the two had the same significance. They were both acted parables, designed to embody truths needful for their instruction as "fishers of men."

But there are differences between the two that are too striking to be undesigned. The first miracle was at the opening of Christ's ministry, the second at its close. The one presents the work of the church during its continuance in the world's history; the other, its welcome at the close of that history, when the work of redemption is finished. The one exhibits the history of the church visible, in its progress through time; the other, the history of the church invisible, as it shall be gathered at last on the shores of eternity. This is no novelty of interpretation, but as old as Augustine, who unfolds repeatedly, with his wonted richness of illustration, this view of the two miracles.

We have then an explanation of the differences in the two cases. In the first miracle Christ was in the ship; in the second, on the shore. In the first, the fish were caught and placed in the ship; in the second, on the shore. In the first, the nets brake, and many escaped to the sea again; in the second, although there were so many, it is distinctly recorded that the nets did not break. In the first, the ship was ready to sink because of the great weight; in the second, there was no danger or alarm of any kind, all was secure.

These differences describe the precise difference between the church militant, and the church triumphant. Now, the church is like a fisher's bark, with its net in the sea. All around her is wild, restless, and troubled. The world is like the ever tossing sea, now calm and quiet, then torn with tempests, and casting up mire and filth. This frail bark of the church is not idle, but busily at work with its nets. And men are gathered within their folds, though of a mixed character, bad as well as good, and the nets themselves are often torn with schism and separation, and of those that are brought into the church, many are but a dead weight, and only tend to swamp and sink her. So it has ever been, so it is now. Those who have seen the church labouring in the wild tossings of human history, have often predicted her destruction. These predictions would have been verified but for one blessed fact, Christ was in the vessel, and she could not be lost. Tossed though she may be, with torn net, and a sinking hull, to human eyes, she cannot perish, for she carries Jesus, and must therefore come safely at last to the shore.

Her condition, when the voyage of time is ended, is vividly presented in the second miracle. There Christ stands to give her a welcome on the quiet shore, giving assurance that when her long night of toil has ended, when her earthly history has closed, she shall be welcomed to that bright and heavenly strand; when with the light of the eternal morning on the hills, she will be brought safely to the shore, not a twine of her net snapped, not a spar shattered, not a purpose or promise of God concerning her unfulfilled or broken. The church visible has torn nets, broken spars, and sinking hulls, for she includes the bad as well as the good; the church invisible has none of these, for she includes only "the sacramental host of God's elect," the redeemed and ransomed, of whom none shall ever be lost.

By the same principle do we interpret the other variations in the miracles. In the first, the net was simply cast in the deep; in the second, on the *right side* of the ship. The right side is the side of honour and value, and it is implied that all who are taken there are good. The same fact is intimated in the numbers taken. In the first, it was a great multitude, uncounted; in the second, one hundred and fifty and three, carefully counted, in spite of the delay thus caused, and all of them great fishes. This difference points not obscurely to the fact that the church visible is composed of a mixed multitude; whilst the church invisible is composed only of that counted number that shall be found in the Lamb's book of life, all of them chosen vessels, counted jewels, sheep known by name to the great Shepherd. Whether the number one hundred and fifty-three has a special significance, may be questioned. Jerome states that it was the precise number of species of fish then known to the ancients, quoting an ancient authority to that effect, and suggests that it was thus intimated that all classes should be found in the number of the saved, and that from every kindred, and tongue, and people, should at last be gathered ransomed souls, by the blood of Christ, and the toils of the church. However this may be, it is obvious that the uncounted mass of the first draught fitly represents the mixed multitude that compose the church visible, whilst the carefully counted and recorded number of the second suggests the chosen seed, the hundred and forty and four thousand that shall stand beside the Lamb on Mount Zion.

Here then we reach the meaning of the fire and food on the

shore. They do not appear in the first miracle, because the church in the periods there represented had not reached her rest. But at the time exhibited in the second she shall be welcomed to that blessed festival—that marriage supper of the Lamb, where there shall sit down in the heavenly kingdom, Abraham, Isaac, and Jacob, with the great company that no man can number. This glorious banquet of heavenly bliss was fitly shadowed forth by the fire of coals, and fish thereon, and bread, that welcomed the weary apostles in the chilly morning that succeeded their night of toil. But why bring of the fish they had caught, to add to this prepared provision? Why, but to shadow forth the great fact that the works of earth shall constitute a part of the joys of heaven. "Blessed are the dead who die in the Lord, for their works shall follow them." Heaven is the gift of God through our Lord Jesus Christ, but the grade and grandeur of that gift will depend on the fidelity with which we toil at the oar and the net in life. The great truth thus presented by the adding of the fish in the net to those on the shore is, that we must carry a part of our heaven with us from earth. It must begin here, or it will not be enjoyed there. Hence the absurdity of hoping that we may live as we please in this life, and yet be allowed to enter at death upon the enjoyments of the life to come. We must carry some part of the heavenly banquet with us. The memories of our efforts to serve God, the words and deeds of love on earth, the souls that have been given us as stars in our crown of rejoicing—all these will constitute a large part of the enjoyments of heaven. When we think how rich must be the rewards that greet such men as Martyn, Whitefield, Payson, and others, who have turned many souls to righteousness, in tracing the results of their labours on earth, in meeting the hundreds that have been brought by their agency to the cross, we can see how fitly this fact was exhibited, by the significant addition that was made to the morning meal on the shore of Galilee.

Hence to the toiling and struggling church, this scene is full of beautiful instruction. She is toiling now in the midst of the sea, and the night is dark on the waters. Much of her toil seems fruitless and thankless, and but few come to her solemn feasts. These unsuccessful efforts are often thrown in her teeth with a taunt, as if they were a mark of her imbecility. We would turn from these words of bitter reproach, and listen to those sweet accents that come through the dim haze that hangs over the waters: "Children, have ye any meat?" and steering by that voice we would press on with the assurance that soon the long night will be gone, and the morning begin to light up the hills, and then shall this weary toil be forgotten, as we are welcomed to the glorious repast that is waiting for us on the shore.

To the individual Christian it also gives most cheering comfort. We too are often toiling all night, and taking nothing. We are ready to despair, because of our want of success. But let us patiently toil on, for there is near us, unseen, one who will give us aid at the right time. Soon the day shall dawn, and the shadows flee away, and on that dim line of sea and shore, where there meet and touch, a tossing time and an unmoving eternity, we shall find one awaiting us, who has said, "When thou passest through the waters, I will be with thee." We know not how we shall meet this last hour, but this we know, that if we are in the ship, we shall find, *as soon as we land*, a joyous greeting, and a feast prepared, of which that cheerful fire and welcome meal on the lonely shore of Galilee, was a significant foreshadowing. Earth will scarce have faded from the dying eye, before heaven, with its undying splendours, shall welcome the weary voyager to its quiet rest. Oh! what a contrast to those who refuse to enter the ark, who also shall be cast on this silent shore of eternity, but not to meet a fire of coals and food thereon, but a fire that shall never be quenched, a lake whose wild tossings of wrath shall continue for ever!

CHAPTER 11

THE SEVENTH APPEARANCE—LOVEST THOU ME?

Peter reinvested with the apostolic office—The fire of coals. I. *The Questions.*
(1) The name by which Peter was addressed. (2) The two words for love. (3)
The contrast with the other disciples. (4) The gradual relenting of Jesus to
Peter. II. *The charges.* Feeding and governing the flock—No primacy of Peter
here—The girding of old age. III. *Lessons from this scene.* (1) The essence of
the Christian life is love to Christ. (2) The test of love is obedience—The German pastor and the picture. (3) Love to Christ is made perfect through
suffering—The girdings and carryings of the Christian—Not loving Christ—
Maranatha.

> "Do not I love thee, dearest Lord?
>   Behold my heart and see;
> And turn the dearest idol out
>   That dares to rival thee.
>
> Is not thy name melodious still
>   To my attentive ear?
>   Doth not each pulse with pleasure bound
>   My Saviour's voice to hear?
>
> Hast thou a lamb in all thy flock
>   I would disdain to feed?
> Hast thou a foe before whose face
>   I fear thy cause to plead?
>
> Thou knowest I love thee, dearest Lord,
>   But oh! I long to soar
> Far from the sphere of mortal joys,
>   And learn to love thee more."

"So when they had dined, Jesus said to Simon Peter, Simon, son
of Jonas, lovest thou me more than these? He saith unto him, Yea,
Lord; thou knowest that I love thee. He saith unto him, Feed my
lambs. He saith to him again the second time, Simon, son of Jonas,
lovest thou me? He saith unto him, Yea, Lord; thou knowest that I
love thee. He saith unto him, Feed my sheep. He saith unto him the

third time, Simon, son of Jonas, lovest thou me? Peter was grieved because he said unto him the third time, Lovest thou me? And he said unto him, Lord, thou knowest all things; thou knowest that I love thee. Jesus saith unto him, Feed my sheep. Verily, verily, I say unto thee, When thou wast young, thou girdedst thyself, and walkedst whither thou wouldest: but when thou shalt be old, thou shalt stretch forth thy hands, and another shall gird thee, and carry thee whither thou wouldest not. This spake he, signifying by what death he should glorify God. And when he had spoken this, he saith unto him, Follow me."—John 21.15—19.

The miracle on the sea and shore of Galilee had a general significance for the whole church. But it had a special meaning for Peter. As the first miracle was designed to introduce Peter to the apostolic office, and give him such instruction as he needed; the second was designed to mark his reinvestment with the office, after the forfeiture of it made by his fall. His personal faith was restored on the first day, during the interview with our Lord, but an official as well as a personal restoration was necessary. This official reinvestment took place on this occasion, and was perhaps the main design of this appearance on the shore. Hence, after the morning repast was over, Peter was specially addressed, and after his formal confession of penitence and faith, was formally reinvested with the apostolic office.

We know not that there was a designed connection in one fact recorded, but it is at least worthy of remark that the last time this evangelist mentions that Peter saw "a fire of coals," was in the palace of the High Priest, when he was guilty of that sad fall, which made this reinvestment of office necessary. Hence, when he saw "a fire of coals," and the form of Jesus near it, the scene in the palace of the High Priest, with his cowardly denial, would naturally rise to his memory, and crimson his cheek with sorrow and shame. But, however this may be, it was soon evident that this interview had a special significance for Peter. After the social repast was over, and the disciples were placed somewhat at their ease, our Lord propounded a question three times to Peter, and each time followed the answer with a charge, from both of which lessons of instruction may be learned.

1. *The questions.*

There are several points that strike us in these questions, thrice repeated by our Lord.

(1) *The name by which Peter was addressed.* It was not Peter, the apostolic name, but that by which he was called before his apostleship, "Simon, son of Jonas." He received his name Cephas, or, in its Greek form, Peter, because of his confession of Christ; but having denied that confession, the name was denied to him. Hence in this tacit refusal to give him his apostolic name, there was an implied rebuke of the severest character, and something that reminded him very vividly of that shameful denial when he forfeited at once his name and his office.

(2) *In the words employed to describe Peter's feelings.* There are two words in the Greek language describing affection, both of which are used in this passage. The one signifies rather a feeling of regard, the other of affection.* The way in which these words are used seems to preclude the possibility of its being accidental. The colder word is used by our Lord in his question, "Simon, son of Jonas, dost thou regard me more than these?" In the selection of this colder term he thus intimated that his love might have sunk even below the feeling of regard. Peter in his reply uses the warmer word, and

---

*This distinction between AGAPAO and PHILEO is not admitted by some scholars. Trench denies it in his *Miracles*, and admits it in his *Synonyms*, N.T. Liddell and Scott state distinctly that AGAPAO differs from PHILEO strictly as implying *regard* and *satisfaction* rather than *affection*. The Passage from Xenophon Memorabilia II. 7. & 9 seems to establish this distinction. Speaking of relatives, Socrates says, "You will love (PHILESEIS) them, when you see that they are serviceable to you, and they will grow attached to you (AGAPESOUSIN)."

affirms that he not only had a *regard* for Jesus, but a *love* for him.

(3) *The contrast suggested with the other disciples.* "Lovest thou me more than *these?*" It is true that the word "these" is ambiguous, and may be referred to either persons or things, as our Lord is supposed to have pointed to the disciples, or the nets, fish, &c. But Peter had never shown any undue love of his worldly business to call for a rebuke, nor was he in any apparent danger of this sin. It is true that Peter could not tell whether his love exceeded that of the other disciples, but our Lord asked not for the fact, but for his opinion. He had expressed the opinion that such was the fact, when he said, "Though all men forsake thee, yet will not I." Then he thought he loved Christ more than the others, and then Christ warned him of his coming fall. Now when Jesus would thrice restore him, from his thrice repeated fall, he reminds him of his former opinion, and asks him if he now thinks that he had even more *regard* for him than the other disciples.

Peter appeals to Christ's own knowledge, and using the warmer word, affirms that he had not only a *regard* for him, but that he *loved* him. But he shrinks from comparing himself now with others, and does not allude to that part of our Lord's question. He had learned a sorrowful wisdom from the past, that prevented him from speaking as he once did.

(4) *The gradual change of Jesus toward him.* This change is shown first in the omission of the painful reference to others in the second question. He stills retains the colder word, but implies that he is satisfied with Peter on the point of his feelings to the other disciples. Peter again replies, using the warmer word to describe his affection.

In the third query, our Lord concedes tacitly Peter's feelings, by adopting the warmer word "love," in asking the question, as if he was satisfied on this point. Peter was grieved because the threefold question not only seemed to doubt the sincerity of his avowals, but pointed plainly to his threefold denial, and brought that scene painfully before his mind. But if Peter was grieved, we may be glad, for we have thus a new confession of his faith, and a testimony to the divinity of the Saviour, in the words, "Lord, *thou knowest all things*, thou knowest that I love thee." This plain ascription of Omniscience to our Lord, and his admission of it by his silence, form an argument for the divinity of Christ, that cannot be evaded without charging both Jesus and Peter with blasphemy. And the fact that the questioning did not cease until this confession was called forth, gives additional strength to the inference that we draw from this declaration, that our Lord was, in very deed, God manifest in the flesh, the divine, omniscient Redeemer.

2. *The charges.*

After each reply of Peter to the query, "Lovest thou me?" our Lord charged him to feed his lambs, or his sheep. There are two words employed here in the Greek, that differ in significance. The first * means to feed, the second† has a wider meaning, and includes the entire work of the shepherd, ruling and superintending the flock, as well as furnishing them with food. These words are hardly used indiscriminately. The first charge is, "Feed my lambs;" the second is, "Shepherd my sheep;" the third, "Feed my sheep." The two words include the two parts of ministerial duty, *instruction* and *government*, and describe the whole pastoral work. The observable fact is that in his charge to the newly invested apostle, our Lord uses the command, "to feed" twice, and to govern but once. Why was this? It would seem plainly to set forth the fact that the great duty of the minister of Jesus is to preach the Word, and to furnish the people with instruction, and that the function of government is subordinate to that of instruction in its prominence and importance. How needful this truth was, all subsequent history establishes. It is the ten-

---

* bosko.   †poimaino

dency of all false systems of religion to generate priestcraft and ghostly rule, because it is the tendency of the unsanctified heart to grasp power. This tendency has been especially manifest in that apostate church, which, as if in judicial blindness of self-condemnation, has called itself by the name of Peter. That church, in the face of this charge of the Lord, has elevated the governing and liturgical office of the minister above that of preaching and instructing, and thus reversed the words of Jesus. It would seem, in foresight of this grasp at priestly power, that our Lord, in giving Peter his apostolic charge, twice commands him to feed, and but once to govern.

Hence it is plain how little support is here furnished for the figment of the primacy of Peter. This reinvestment of office and charge have sometimes been used for that purpose, but in flagrant disregard of the whole teaching of the scene. Our Lord does not appoint him chief shepherd on earth, but only reinstates him in an office he had lost by his fall. The absurdity of this claim is apparent from the fact that Peter, thirty years after this time, when writing his epistle, gives the same charge to the elders of the church, and expressly disavows all primacy. "The elders which are among you, I exhort, who am also an elder, and a witness of the sufferings of Christ—feed* the flock of God, which is among you, taking the oversight (the episcopacy) thereof—neither as being lords over God's heritage." 1 Pet. 5.1-3. Using the same word to describe their official work that our Lord does in describing his, he transfers to all these elders whatever power Christ bestowed on him in the use of this word, and accompanies this with a warning against priestly domination.

We have then, in this thrice-repeated restoration to office, a precise correspondence to the thrice-repeated fall, and a delineation of the nature of the ministerial work. It is an office of teaching and ruling, but the great function of it is to

---

* poimanate

preach the gospel. In doing this, the pastor must begin with the lambs, instruct and secure the instruction of the young, then instruct and rule discreetly the more advanced, so that each one may receive his food in due season, and he should remember always that he holds and uses his office not for his own good, but for the good of others.

Having sketched the work of his life, our Lord then indicates the nature of his death. "When thou wast young, thou girdedst thyself, &c." This we are assured was an intimation that, after the toil of a long life, he must end that life with the death of a martyr. Indeed we have reason to believe that at least this portion of the Gospel of John was written after the death of Peter, and hence the prominence given to this prediction. Many years passed before this prophecy was fulfilled, but tradition affirms that at last it was verified, and this strong-hearted apostle ended his career on the cross. But it is also affirmed that he begged the privilege, which was granted to him, of being crucified with his head downward, feeling unworthy of the privilege of suffering precisely like his beloved Master. Thus was it literally fulfilled, that when he was old, he stretched forth his hands, and another girded him and carried him whither he would not. And we cannot doubt that, as the mists of death gathered over his eyes, the same form that appeared on the lonely hills of Galilee was revealed again, and that as he neared the shore of eternity, he saw, not a fire of coals and fish thereon, but the radiant scenes of that city that hath foundations, where he was welcomed to the rest that remaineth for the people of God.

Having delivered this prophecy in words, our Lord embodied it in a symbolical act, and moving up the rocky shore said to Peter, "Follow me."

3. *Lessons from this scene.*

(1) *The essence of the Christian life is love to Christ.* Love to God and man is the fulfilling of the law; love to the God-man, the divine and yet human Saviour, is the essence of the

gospel. So it was with Peter as these questions proved, and so it must be with us. We too have denied Christ. Impenitence is a constant denial of him, a constant asseveration, "I am not his disciple." There is nothing of which the impenitent man is more ashamed than of acknowledging that he is anxious about his soul. His life is a denial of Jesus. Nor does this always cease when he enters the church. The Christian professor often denies his Master, and conceals his profession, or makes some unworthy compromise with the world.

Then it may be that Jesus comes to him after some season of darkness and sorrow, and whispers comfort to his soul, and even makes the rocky shore to glow with rich provision for his wants, and then whispers in his ear, "Lovest thou me?"

If the dealings of God have been sanctified to his soul, he will have an humble spirit, a spirit that will not claim superiority over other disciples, but only say with lowly and yet fervent sincerity, "Thou knowest that I love thee."

He will have a penitent spirit that is not only grieved for sin in the past, but resolved to avoid it in the future. And he will also have a drawing of his heart to Jesus, so that though he can only reach him by wading through the deep waters, or climbing the rugged hills, he will strive to get nearer to him, feeling that the love of Christ constrains him, and that his life is now love.

(2) *The test of love is obedience.* "If ye love me, keep my commandments," was only another form of the same test that our Lord gave to Peter when he said, "Feed my sheep." There is a love that vents itself in rapture and ecstasy, which may be a spurious excitement. The test is, Do you work for Christ? He is not on earth in person, but he has many representatives. The lambs and the sheep are always with us, and we can always show our love for him by our attention to them. This matter shall be made the subject of inquiry again when it shall be said to many, "Inasmuch as ye did it not to the least of these, ye did it not to me." Hence if we would know

whether we love the Saviour, let us feed his lambs, let us go and seek out the poor, the sick, and the sorrowing; and as we toil for them, because they are Christ's feeble ones, we shall find our own love grow stronger and be able to say with deep sincerity, "Lord, thou knowest all things, thou knowest that I love thee."

A pastor in Germany, who had been somewhat neglectful of his duty, was asked to dine one day with a friend, and after dinner chanced to see a picture that riveted his attention. It was a representation of the crucified Redeemer, with the words coming from his lips, "All this I did for thee, what doest thou for me?" It was a voice from heaven to his conscience, and he went home with the words ringing in his ears, "What doest thou for me?" and from that day he began to labour for Christ, with a zeal that knew no pause until he was able to say, "Lord Jesus, receive my spirit."

Should these words come to you, O reader, from the Lamb slain in the midst of the throne, and if the thought of all his weariness and agony, his tears and toils, his life and death, came up to you, to tell what he did for you, what could you then adduce—what toils, what sacrifices, what work, would come up in memorial of what you were doing for him? If you love him, keep his commandments: if you love him, go forth and feed his flock, both sheep and lambs.

(3) *Love for Christ is made perfect by suffering.* "Verily, verily, I say unto thee, when thou wast young, thou girdedst thyself and walkedst whither thou wouldest; but when thou shalt be old, thou shalt stretch forth thy hands, and another shall gird thee, and carry thee whither thou wouldest not." In early life the soul is wilful in its unsubdued strength, and the will unbending. Youth is proud of its stirring powers, and walks with an unbowed neck. But if we continue to follow Christ, we shall learn the lesson of denying self, and giving up our own wills to the will of God. Others shall gird us and carry us whither we would not. We shall be carried to a sick

bed, to a post of toilsome labour, to a house of mourning, or to a place of suffering; but the blessed fact is that Christ is there, and our love for him is never perfected until it has been purified by suffering. So was it with the fervid writer of this gospel. He loved Christ when he was willing to call fire from heaven on the Samaritans, to rebuke the miracle worker who followed not him, and wished to take a place at the right hand of the Messiah in his triumph. But that love never reached its sublimest fervour until half a century of suffering enabled him to pour forth those lines of seraphic love that sparkle and glow in the loving epistles in which he has recorded the emotions of his heart.

So was it also with Peter. It was in his old age, on the very verge of martyrdom, that he wrote those epistles, which hang rich and glowing with the ripe clusters of a love made perfect through sufferings. It may not be for us to witness for Christ as Peter did, at the stake of martyrdom; but we may just as truly witness for him in the chamber of sickness, the house of mourning, the hovel of poverty, and the dreariness of disappointment and bereavement; and in this manly witnessing, our love shall become as gold seven times refined, or as the rich and blushing clusters of fruit that are reddest and ripest because they have been subjected to the hottest sun. Then if suffering in any form be our lot, let us remember that the Captain of our salvation was made perfect through sufferings; that Peter and John, and the great cloud of witnesses, trod the same pathway; and that there are unfoldings of our Christian character that never take place until suffering comes, just as there are fruits that never ripen until touched by the frost.

But we cannot conclude this chapter, without adverting to the fact, that it may have some reader, who in answer to the query, "Lovest thou me?" must say, "Lord, thou knowest that I *do not* love thee." And the fearful words that are written about such an one are, "If any man love not the Lord Jesus

Christ, let him be anathema maranatha." Yes, "maranatha," the Lord cometh! There comes a time when you, poor, drifting voyager, shall end this lonely voyage, on a lonelier shore. A blacker night shall hang over the waters than that which rested on deep Galilee, and a sterner shore shall meet your startled gaze than the rocky strand of Gennesaret. It will be the blackness of darkness for ever, the awful reality of an unblest and unforgiven eternity. We know not the forms and the sights that shall meet you on that wild and mysterious shore. We know not the words that shall break first on your astonished ear. But we do know that, unless you die at peace with God through our Lord Jesus Christ, you shall awake in that unknown land to shame and everlasting contempt, and find that you are shipwrecked in your hopes for eternity.

CHAPTER 12

THE SEVENTH APPEARANCE—WHAT IS THAT TO THEE?

The walk on the shore—silent love—uncertainty of tradition—The breathing grave. I. *The question*. Peter's possible motives. (1) A momentary pang of repining—The feelings of the afflicted—A target for the Almighty. (2) Mere curiosity—Intimacy of Peter and John—Anxiety to pry into the future— Wisdom of the veil that hides it. II. *The answer*. (1) The events of life ordered by the will of God—Predestination a doctrine full of comfort. (2) The Christian's life on earth a tarrying for the summons home—The aged and invalid— The dairyman's daughter. (3) The cure of all anxiety for the future is the discharge of present duty—Follow Jesus.

> " 'Follow me,' I know thy voice;
> Jesus, Lord, thy steps I see;
> Now I take thy yoke by choice;
> Light thy burden now to me."

"Then Peter, turning about, seeth the disciple whom Jesus loved following, which also leaned on his breast at supper, and said, Lord, which is he that betrayeth thee? Peter seeing him, saith to Jesus, Lord, and what shall this man do? Jesus saith unto him, If I will that he tarry till I come, what is that to thee? follow thou me."—John 21.20—22.

This is the third scene in this remarkable interview on the shore of Tiberias. It would seem that our Lord, after restoring Peter to his apostleship by the threefold question and answer, began to move along the shore, and commanded Peter to follow him. This command was not a mere injunction to imitate him, but part of an acted scene, full of instruction. To foreshadow that rugged path of life that Peter was to tread, our Lord began to ascend the steep and rocky shore, and commanded the restored apostle to follow him. Peter, having learned the lesson of obedience by the sad scenes of the past, instantly obeyed him, and rough though the path was, did not refuse to tread it, when he was only following in the footsteps of Jesus.

They had proceeded but a short distance when, hearing a step behind them, Peter turned and saw John, it would seem, also following Jesus. There is something characteristically beautiful in this silent act of the beloved disciple. Jesus had not commanded him to follow, but when he saw Christ go forward, he could not stay behind; for his heart clung too fondly to both the Master and the disciple, to allow him to remain. It is as if he had said in his heart, The path may be rugged, but where Jesus leads, there I will follow. This is a striking illustration of that deep, silent, loving obedience of John, as contrasted with the unrestrained impulsiveness of Peter. Peter, instead of quietly following Jesus, as he was bidden, looked back, and instead of minding his own footsteps, minded those of John, and asked, Lord, and what shalt this man do? Our Lord, in rebuke to this feeling thus expressed, replied, "If I will that he tarry till I come, what is that to thee? Follow thou me."

It is recorded that from this, the saying went forth that John was not to die. The utter uncertainty of tradition as a rule of interpreting scripture is most strikingly illustrated here. Tradition interpreted these words of our Lord as an assurance that John would not die, though the tradition was made during the lives of inspired men. So extensive was this error, that it was needful to correct it by inspiration itself. But so tenacious was it, that even this correction did not wholly remove it, for when John did actually die, many believed that his death was not real, but only a trance or sleep, and some said that the earth could be seen moving on his grave, with the gentle breathing of the sleeper below. So wide-spread was this error, that even Augustine, in the fourth century, did not wholly reject it as false. Hence, when the followers of Peter, as they strangely term themselves, in both Rome and Oxford, tell us that we must rely on tradition as the rule by which scripture is to be interpreted, we have only to point to the scene in Galilee to show that, by the testimony of Scripture itself, tradition is fallacious, for even among inspired men and in a single generation it had so widely erred as to require a special revelation to correct it. If under such favourable circumstances it could not be trusted, how utterly untrustworthy must it be when it reaches us through fifty generations of superstition and error?

There are two things that arrest our attention in this scene: the question, and the answer.

1. *The question*, "Lord, and what shall this man do?"

In the Greek, the words "shall do" are not found, and the question is simply "Lord, but this man, what?" That is, How shall it be with him? How shall he die? Shall it be as I am to die? That this is his meaning appears plainly from the reply of Jesus. He had just told Peter that his life must be one of obedience through scenes of suffering, and his death one of violence. When he saw John following, he presumed that our Lord would also declare how it would be with him, and hence asked the question.

What were the precise motives of Peter in asking this question, we do not certainly know, but we may infer that they were not exactly right, since the answer of our Lord was refusal in the form of a rebuke. We may conjecture several possible motives.

(1) *A momentary pang of repining.* As our Lord lifted the veil from the future to Peter, and showed him the dark and rugged path before him, a path of toil and trial whose end was tinged with blood, we do not wonder that Peter felt a recoil from the prospect. When he turned then to the beloved John, and thought that perhaps no such path was marked for him, the thought may have entered the mind of Peter, that his case was a hard one, and that John also ought to be made to

share this lot. His feeling was, "Am I to be singled out thus for suffering? Are there no words of sad revelation also to him? How is it to be with him in life and in death?" The afflicted know but too well the nature of this feeling. When some great blow has made the heart sad and the home silent, it is not without a pang that the eye can look on those who have not been thus stricken. As the lonely mourner passes along the streets, and sees in the twilight the glow of the evening fires, and hears the sound of happy voices around the hearth, the thought of his solitary chamber, his cheerless home, and his gloomy heart, will come back upon him with a bitter intensity; he will contrast his lonely sadness with their bright joy, and remember that he perhaps was yet more faithful than they in the discharge of duty. And the query will rise, Why are others exempt, whilst I suffer? Why should I be singled out as a target for the arrows of the Almighty? So it may have been with Peter in thus contrasting his rugged lot with that of John.

The feeling, however, was wrong. If it be Christ's will that Peter should suffer and John escape, that will was right, and to be quietly borne. But the fact that John was not to suffer as Peter did, was no proof that he was not to suffer at all. He did suffer, and if Peter was called to a violent death, he was called to an earlier entrance into heaven than the beloved apostle who was left to linger to a feeble old age on earth. Thus is it in the distribution of earthly sorrows. They are not only according to the will of Christ, but they are much more equally distributed than we suppose. There are counterbalancings to both joy and sorrow on earth, by which the result of human happiness, in the case of the true children of God, is made in the end to be equalized in a wonderful manner.

(2) *Mere Curiosity.* Peter was probably a devoted friend of John. They were townsmen; perhaps partners in business; were associated in some of the most remarkable events of the life of our Lord; were together in the Judgment Hall; and

came together to the grave. Hence Peter may, from mere affectionate curiosity, have desired to know what was in reserve for one whom he so much loved.

This feeling is also a very natural one, and often indulged. As we look on the little babe that nestles in our arms, we long to forecast its future, to know whether it will live, and if so, what shall be the complexion of its life. So also in regard to ourselves, we are anxious to know whether we shall be spared to raise our children, whether we shall be rich or poor, in sickness or health, and above all, when or how death shall come to us; and we long to lift the dim veil that hides the future, and read the unopened leaves of our history. But in mercy to us is that veil impenetrable and that volume sealed. Could we read the undeveloped future, the present would lose many if not all its joys, and be deprived of its most precious discipline. The sorrows to come would be all gathered on the present, instead of being diffused over our entire course, and thus darken the joys that we feel now; whilst the faith and trust that are now developed by the perplexities and troubles of the present, would be rendered impossible by the knowledge of the precise issues of the future; and duty which now brings its own reward in the mere exercise of our powers, would lose all its stimulus by the knowledge of its apparent uselessness, in securing the immediate object of its aims. Hence this vain curiosity is all wrong, and should be repressed. We cannot and ought not to lift the veil that hides the future, for it is enough to know that it shall be well with the righteous and ill with the wicked, in the end; and when that end is reached, all the mysterious steps of the way will be clear in the glorious light of eternity. It is for us, simply to follow Jesus.

2. We consider the *answer* of our Lord, "If I will that he tarry till I come, what is that to thee? follow thou me."

The coming here spoken of must be his second coming to judgment, for it was evidently so understood by those who heard it, and John does not correct this opinion in correcting their erroneous inference. He simply calls their attention to the fact that Christ did not say that he should not die, but only, "If I will that he tarry," and thus do not die, "what is that to thee?" The fact that he made no correction of this opinion, implies that he considered it to be true.

There are three thoughts suggested by this reply.

(1) *The events of life are all ordered according to the will of God.* "*If I will* that he tarry, &c." We assume of course that Christ is God, in this statement, for he himself assumes it. God alone has the right thus to speak about life and death, and the use of such language by Jesus is a clear claim of his divine character. The language "*If I will*," implies that the life of John was to be precisely as he willed it should be. Now as this could not be peculiar to John, it asserts a truth common to all, that our lives are all ordered by God, and shall be exactly as his eternal purpose has ordained them to be.

It is strange that the mind of a true Christian should resist a doctrine that carries with it so much light, and breathes into life so much significance, and bestows on it so much value. If our lives are left to mere chance, or simply to our own blind and feeble efforts, we may well be discouraged, for we are too short-sighted and weak to carry them to any great and good end. Especially is this true of the sorrows of life. If these sorrows come by mere accident, and not according to the wise and predetermined purpose of God, they become tenfold more crushing, because they are mere aimless burdens of agony. But if they come by the fore-ordaining will of our heavenly Father, are part of his eternal plan, and all ordained for gracious ends, we are able to bear the stroke, for though we see it not, it is designed in mercy and love.

The same thing is true of the blessings of life. If they come according to no plan, no previous intention of God, it is hard to see how they can demand our gratitude. But coming, as all these things do, by the will and according to the eternal purpose of Jehovah, we see life invested with a high significance, because of the high purpose that informs it. If sorrows and trials come, we are cheered in bearing them by the thought that they are sent, not by the drifting of an aimless chance, but by the hand of a merciful Father. If joys are mingled in our lot, we are grateful to him by whose will they are thus bestowed. If dark clouds hang on the horizon of the future, we can go forward with unfaltering courage, for we know that the future, equally with the past, is embraced in this eternal plan, and that not a hair of our heads shall fall without our heavenly Father. On the rushing railroad train, in the ship on the pathless deep, even in the dread roar of the battle field, there shall nothing befall the child of God in the path of duty, but in accordance with the will of Jesus; and hence he can go forward enfolded with more than a panoply of steel, namely, with the protecting purpose of the Almighty.

(2) *The Christian's life is a tarrying for the summons home.* "If I will that he *tarry*."

The world is not our home, and life to the true child of God is but waiting for the appointed change. As the soldier, the labourer, the traveller, all wait the expected welcome home as the solace for present privations and toils, so is it with the Christian. Waiting, or tarrying, implies that there is something irksome in this position, and that there is a longing to depart, and be with Christ which is far batter. But tarrying by the will of Christ implies that it is not an aimless thing, but an arrangement that is based on wise and holy reasons.

It often happens that the aged, who have outlived all their active usefulness, and have seen those they love drop one by one into the grave, are disposed to ask, Why am I thus left behind? Why am I left as a dead tree in the forest, all stripped and bare? The same thought often harasses the confined and helpless invalid. There is a feeling that the poor sick one is nothing but a burden, capable of giving no pleasure to those around, a mere useless and troublesome weight on those who may perhaps be wishing to be released from the exactions of helpless suffering; and the question often will rise bitterly, Why am I, a poor useless thing, made to tarry here, whilst others, so capable of active exertion, are taken away?

Let not any such feelings be cherished. The aged Christian, though bowed with decrepitude and sorrow, can show how the religion of Jesus can sustain the weary pilgrim when all else is taken away, and can gild the dark horizon of life with the crimson and gold of a glorious sunset, and thus can exhibit the power of Jesus in its most illustrious form, and make the hoary hairs to hang as a crown of light on the brow of age. Nor is the poor invalid useless. From the sick room where a patient piety is enduring suffering with unmurmuring submission, there go forth a thousand gentle lessons of tenderness, of patience, and of charity, that not only demonstrate the power of Christ to sustain when all others fail, but that also have a direct softening influence on the heart. The Dairyman's Daughter[1], from her sick room, has preached to half the world; and though long since in her grave, yet like the grave of Elisha, where the dust of the prophet whom a lingering illness had borne down to the tomb, when it touched the dead body of a man, restored it to life, from the grave of Elizabeth Wallbridge, there has gone forth a virtue denied to many a one who like Elijah has gone up in a chariot of fire to heaven. Then let none repine, if they tarry, for they are doing the will of God, and home at last will be but the sweeter for this season of lingering on the journey.

3. *The cure of all anxieties for the future is the discharge of the duties of the present.* "What is that to thee? *follow thou me.*

The Christian life is summed up in following Christ. We begin it by coming to him, we continue it by following him, we end it by going to him. And the answer to many of the perplexities that beset its entrance and ongoing is simply, Follow Jesus. Is it objected that there are difficult doctrines in the

Bible? Follow Jesus, and they will be found no obstacle in the way. Is it said that professors of religion walk inconsistently? Follow Jesus, and this inconsistency will not be in your way. Are there business relations that trammel? Follow Jesus, and do life's great business, and all these things shall be added unto you. Do you ask leave to go and bury your father? Let the dead bury their dead, follow thou Jesus. Thus to every cavil, or excuse, the one and only reply is, Follow Jesus; and as you go up, the light will grow clearer, and what now perplexes will perplex no longer, and at each step in the journey, the footsteps of Jesus shall irradiate the path. And when that path goes down to the dark valley, even there his presence shall sustain, and on the other side, eternity shall be but a following of Jesus, for the Lamb shall lead us to the fountains of living waters, and God shall wipe away all tears from our eyes.

---

[1]A tract included in *Annals of the Poor* 1814 (Legh Richmond). 4 million copies in 19 languages were in circulation before 1850.

CHAPTER 13

THE EIGHTH APPEARANCE—THE FIVE HUNDRED WITNESSES

I. *Place of this meeting.* Probably the mount of transfiguration—Why in Galilee. II. *Importance of this meeting.* Thrice predicted—A meeting of the whole church then on earth—Preparation for coming conflicts by a revelation of Christ's glory—Why some doubted. III. *Comparative silence of Scripture concerning it.* Reason for this silence—The transfiguration, why so little alluded to—Meeting Jesus on earth—Meeting him hereafter in heaven.

"When I can read my title clear
 To mansions in the skies,
I bid farewell to every fear,
 And wipe my weeping eyes.
Let cares like a wild deluge come
 And storms of sorrow fall,
May I but safely reach my home,
 My God, my heaven, my all."

"After that he was seen of above five hundred brethren at once, of whom the greater part remain unto this present, but some are fallen asleep."—1 Cor. 15.6.

"Then the eleven disciples went away into Galilee into a mountain where Jesus had appointed them. And when they saw him, they worshipped him, but some doubted."—Matt. 28.16,17.

This appearance of our Lord, though a very important one, is but lightly touched upon in the New Testament, and we are left to gather its meaning and circumstances by a careful study of the brief references that are made to it. There can be no reasonable doubt that the appearance to the five hundred, referred to by Paul, and the meeting on the mountain in Galilee, related by Matthew, are the same, for there is no other appearance or meeting with which either can be connected.

Hence we consider them together, and it will be seen that they cast light on each other when carefully pondered. There are several distinct points that claim our consideration.

1. *The Place.* It was a mountain in Galilee. What it was, or why Galilee was selected, must be left to conjecture. But there are reasons that suggest themselves for this meeting in Galilee rather than in any other region. It was in Galilee that Jesus spent the first thirty years of his life, in the obscurity of Nazareth, the obedient son, as he was reputed, of a lowly carpenter. It was in Cana of Galilee that he did his first miracle, and began his mighty works. It was in Galilee that he sat down on a mount, and delivered that wonderful sermon whose precepts and beatitudes, after eighteen centuries, the world is yet unable fully to meet. It was in Galilee that Nazareth, the home of his youth, and Capernaum, the home of his manhood, were found. It was in Galilee that the majority of his disciples were found, so that the very name Galilean became synonymous with that of a follower of Jesus. It was also in Galilee that he was transfigured, and had that memorable interview with Moses and Elias, concerning which Jesus charged them, to "tell the vision to no man, *until the Son of man be risen again from the dead.*" Matt. 17.9.

In these words we believe there lies the clue to the place, the facts, and the meaning of this meeting with the five hundred. The transfiguration scene is connected by our Lord with something subsequent to his resurrection, and this meeting in Galilee is promised after the resurrection, as something of great importance, and there is really nothing after the resurrection to which the implied promise at the transfiguration can be referred, but this meeting with the five hundred. There is a remarkable silence concerning the transfiguration after the resurrection, difficult to explain, unless we suppose that it was linked with this scene as its great counterpart and public announcement to the church. If this scene is thus connected with the transfiguration, all becomes plain and significant.

Other reasons for this opinion will be suggested when we come to look more narrowly at the actual facts of the meeting, but these general reasons will suggest the probability that it was the mount of transfiguration that was selected by our Lord, as the place of this great meeting.

He knew that he had left many devoted and sorrowing disciples in Galilee. Whilst only one hundred and twenty names were found in Jerusalem, more than five hundred were collected in Galilee, and hence Galilee was the most suitable place for this meeting. In Jerusalem they were compelled to meet in secret rooms and upper chambers, at night, by stealth, with locked and guarded doors, for fear of their enemies, and but a few could enjoy the privilege of seeing and hearing their risen Lord. In Galilee were many who, by reason of age, poverty, sex, or other causes, must have been deprived of the direct proof that Jesus had risen, had not this meeting been appointed. Hence it was called by our Lord on this mountain, in Galilee, where in the solitude of its sublime elevation, afar from the noise of men, they might gaze on the form of the beloved Master, and listen to the words of his lips.

Tradition designates Tabor as the mount of transfiguration, but the facts of its populousness, and its distance from Capernaum, make it rather improbable that it was the scene of that wonderful transaction. Whatever was the precise locality, the retirement and silence of the mountain, its elevation and grandeur, as a spot rising up towards heaven, and purified by its breezes and showers, all combined to make it a suitable place for this remarkable meeting. And we cannot but think how often, since, the stricken disciples have thus met amid the mountains of Piedmont, Savoy, Switzerland, and Scotland, and found the glens and fastnesses of the rocks to be places of transfiguration to their souls, where they saw the King in his beauty, and the land that is afar off.

2. *The importance* of this meeting.

That it was important is plain from the facts, that our Lord appointed it the night before he died; that the angels repeated this promise to the women in announcing his resurrection; and that he himself repeated the promise in his interview with them. It was therefore a meeting of great importance, for some reason. If we suppose no unusual appearance of our Lord at that time, we are utterly at fault in trying to discover its importance. But if we suppose a substantial reproduction of the transfiguration scene, its importance and significance are seen at a glance.

The general ground of this importance lies in the fact that this "upwards of five hundred" comprised nearly, if not all, the whole body of believers then on earth. It was Christ's first and last meeting with the whole church on earth, after the incarnation, until he should come the second time, without sin, unto salvation. One reason of this meeting was that the clearest evidence of his resurrection should be given to the largest number, enabling them to see, hear, and touch him in open daylight, when all ocular deception was impossible. This being done, the whole church could testify to the truth of this fundamental fact; and twenty years afterwards Paul was able to appeal to this testimony, and to the fact that a majority of this five hundred were yet alive and able to testify that they had seen the risen Jesus.

But this did not exhaust the meaning of this interview. It seems to have had another object, found in the fact already suggested that it was a kind of transfiguration. The language of Matthew seems to demand this supposition. He tells us that two very opposite effects were produced. Some worshipped, and some doubted. Had it been a mere ordinary appearance, these extraordinary effects of it are hard to explain. But if we suppose an extraordinary appearance, we can see how some would be awed into adoration, and others bewildered into doubt, by the august spectacle presented. As Jesus had sealed the lips of Peter, James, and John, *until* he was risen from the dead, it was to be expected that *when* thus risen the announcment would be made, and if not made here we have no record of it having been done for nearly half a century. But if we suppose that the seal was then removed, and that the three apostles declared that on this same spot they had seen the excellent glory, and heard the voice of the Father saying, "This is my beloved Son in whom I am well pleased," and that hence this glorious divine being, all radiant with the light of heaven, was truly the same lowly and gentle teacher that they had before known and loved, all becomes plain. Those who received the words of the apostle would fall down and worship him with grateful adoration as the Son of God. But those who were dazzled with this glory, might doubt whether this form of unearthly majesty were truly the same that walked the dusty streets of the city, or sat at the margin of the well in hunger, thirst, and weariness, the "man of sorrows and acquainted with grief."

In the same supposed fact, we find the grand significance of the transaction. The first transfiguration was designed to strengthen our Lord for "the decease that he was to accomplish at Jerusalem." The vision of heavenly glory, and the words of heavenly love that Moses and Elias brought, strengthened him by the joy that was set before him to endure the cross, despising the shame. But now he was about to depart to that glory, and leave his disciples to toil, trial, and suffering. Some of them were feeble in faith, as their very doubts indicate. It was then needful for them to have something to strengthen that faith, and enable them to endure the trials before them. What more likely to do both, than a glimpse of that glory which they would share, when called to meet him on the streets of the heavenly city? As they gazed on that radiant form, they would behold, in its heavenly beauty and brightness, a picture of what awaited them, when, after a little season of toil, this vile body should be made like to his glorious body, and they should see him as he is. Hence we cannot wonder that some, as they gazed, began to exult with rapture, and bent the knee in adoring worship, and uttered the first notes of that song, which, begun on earth, is never ended in heaven; whilst others, bewildered, amazed, feeling that it was too glorious a vision to be real, too wonderful a hope for such poor, perishing creatures as they, should doubt. But in the scene itself thus supposed, we see the wonderful love of Jesus in thus furnishing them so richly for the trials before them, by this blessed vision of the glory that awaited them.

3. Another point remains to be considered, *the comparative silence of Scripture concerning this important meeting.*

It is remarkable that a meeting like this, so important that it was three times predicted, should not be recorded at length, whilst other meetings, not thus predicted, are thus recorded. It seems strange at first sight that Paul should allude to it, whilst John and James do not.

This fact will also find its explanation in what has been suggested as the grand object of the meeting. Had this meeting been designed to establish facts that were for the entire church, it would have been recorded more minutely, and more special reference been given to it. But it was in some respects like the transfiguration, and occupies a similar place in the subsequent revelations of Scripture. It is a remarkable fact, that an event so wonderful as that of the transfiguration, should have so little allusion made to it in the writings of the apostles. The reason of this is found in the fact that the great object of the transfiguration terminated in the mind of our Lord himself. It was mainly designed to prepare him for his approaching sufferings, and having accomplished this end, we find but little subsequent reference to it. So was it also with the event before us. It was designed mainly to prepare the church for the storm that was soon to burst upon it, and to cheer the hearts of Christians by a vision of the glory that awaited them. It was not therefore necessary that it should be written at length in a book, for it was already indelibly written on the memories of those for whose sake it was particularly revealed. The very fact that it was enacted before so many witnesses, made it less necessary to put it on record, for the knowledge of the facts would be diffused sufficiently, without such a record. Private appearances of our Lord were sometimes more fully recorded, for the very reason that they were private, and could only be satisfactorily known in this way. But public appearances like this, whose main design was to act upon the living, were not fully recorded, because their very publicity made it less necessary to publish them in this way. Hence we have the simple fact that they happened, and nothing to satisfy mere curiosity.

It is enough for us to know that there is a mount of ordinances where we too may meet Jesus, and see him in his glory by the eye of faith. As we retire from the world and ascend that mount, in the quiet of solitary prayer, or in the communings of the great congregation, we too may have precious glimpses of him whom our souls love. And as we visit his sepulchre, we too may hear his promise to meet us again, not on the rocks and hills of Palestine, or even on the mount of transfiguration there; not with the five hundred witnesses, where doubting and tears mingled with worship and gladness; but on those hills of light that stretch away over the heavenly Canaan; in that city that hath no need of the sun or the moon to lighten it, and among the ten thousand times ten thousand, and thousands of thousands, that stand around the throne; where all tears shall be wiped away, all sorrow forgotten, and where we shall sing the song of eternal victory through him that loved us, and gave himself for us. Let us prepare for this glorious meeting, for he has gone before us, not into Galilee, but into heaven.

THE NINTH APPEARANCE—
JAMES THE LORD'S BROTHER

The three Jameses—James the Just, the brother of our Lord—His character by
Hegesippus—Apocryphal traditions—His childhood and Nazaritic dedication—Not a disciple of Jesus at first—His position in the church—The significance of this appearance to him—The silence of Scripture—General teachings.

> "Till God in human flesh I see,
>   My thoughts no comfort find,
> The holy, just, and sacred Three,
>   Are terrors to my mind.
>
> While Jews on their own law rely,
>   And Greeks of wisdom boast,
> I love the incarnate mystery,
>   And there I fix my trust."

"After that he was seen of James." 1 Cor. 15.7

There are several persons mentioned in the New Testament
under the name of James. The most prominent in the gospels
is James the son of Zebedee and brother of John, who was the
first martyr among the apostles. There was another James
among the twelve, called James, the son of Alpheus, who is
called in one place, (Mark 15.40,) James the less, alluding to
inferiority of age or of stature to the son of Zebedee. There is
mention in the Epistles and Gospels, of James the brother of
our Lord, and it is a very difficult question to determine
whether he is the same person called the son of Alpheus, or
another. Neander pronounces this one of the most difficult
questions in apostolic history. The more probable opinion is
that he was different from the son of Alpheus, and was not

one of the twelve apostles, nor indeed, in the first instance, a
follower of Jesus at all. In John 7.5, it is stated that "neither
did his brethren believe in him;" and in Matt. 13.55, and
Mark 6.3, James is mentioned as one of the brethren of our
Lord, and the mode in which they are named seems to intimate that they were not at that time his avowed disciples.
Our Lord confirms this where he says, (Matt. 13.57,) "A
prophet is not without honour, save in his own country, and
in his own house." Hence the conclusion that seems most
probable is, that James the brother of our Lord, was distinct
from the son of Alpheus, was not one of the twelve apostles,
nor indeed a disciple of Jesus at all during the early part of his
ministry, but became one before his death; and afterwards,
(whether strictly an apostle or not, may be doubtful,) was an
apostolic man of great eminence, the Moderator of the first
Synod in Jerusalem, first pastor of the church there, and
author of the Epistle that bears his name. It was undoubtedly
to this James that our Lord appeared, for he is the only one
mentioned by Paul in his epistles, and is expressly called (Gal.
1.19) "the brother of the Lord." By gathering the scattered
rays of light that are left regarding him, we may obtain some
notion of the object of this appearance.

We have, from traditional sources, some facts that are reliable about James, and others that are obviously mixed with
fable. He is called James the Just, because of the saintly austerity of his character, an austerity so high and spotless as to
exact the reverence of the Jewish people to a very great
degree. Hegesippus, a Jewish Christian of the second century,
tells us that James led, from his youth, a life of the most exem-
plary strictness. He states that he was holy from his mother's
womb; that no razor ever came on his head; that he never
anointed himself with oil, nor used the bath; that he wore no
woollen, but only linen clothes, like the priests; that he only of
the Christians was allowed to enter the holy of holies, and
that he was so much in the temple on his knees, in prayer for

his people, that his knees became hard like a camel's, and that he was called Obliam, the bulwark of the people. (Eusebius, Eccles. Hist. 2-23.) He further assures us that he was martyred, about A. D. 69, by being cast from the pinnacle of the temple, and stoned by the Pharisees, crying with his latest breath, "I pray thee, Lord God, Father, forgive them! for they know not what they do." Eusebius adds that some of the most intelligent of the Jews believed that the destruction of Jerusalem took place soon after because of his cruel murder.

The apocryphal Gospel to the Hebrews mentions this appearance of our Lord to James, but mingles it with evident fable. It states that, "After Jesus had given the shroud to the servant of the high priest, he went to James. James had made a vow, after partaking of the bread given by Christ at the last supper, that he would eat no more until he had seen Jesus risen from the dead; Jesus coming to him, had a table with bread brought out, blessed the bread, and gave it to James, with the words, 'Eat thy bread now, my brother, since the Son of Man has risen from the dead.' " This is evidently fabulous, for it makes our Lord appear to an unbeliever, and appear very soon after his resurrection to James; whereas the gospels never allude to any appearance made to an unbeliever, and Paul directly asserts that the appearance to James was after that to the five hundred, and hence after the first eight appearances, which carries us onward near the close of the forty days. But it shows the early conviction of the church that it was to this James that the appearance was made, and that it was with a purpose of kindness to him that it was done.

Looking at all these facts, we are able to gather a very distinct notion of this austere and saintly man—of his history and character, of his place in the apostolic church, and of the reason why our Lord afforded to him, as he did to Peter and Thomas, a special interview.

It is not necessary to discuss the question whether James was the son of Joseph by a former marriage, or the son of

Mary, and the full brother of our Lord. It would seem that he was dedicated from the womb by a Nazaritic vow. Perhaps the peculiar circumstances connected with the birth of Jesus, and John the Baptist, led to this solemn dedication of James. Being thus devoted to God, his education was peculiarly Jewish, and he grew up with an intense devotion to the Mosaic law. This rigid Judaism made the peculiar doctrines of Jesus distasteful to him, and prevented him from believing that Jesus was the Christ. He could not at first see how the man who ate with publicans and sinners, could be the holy one of God; or how one whom he had known in childhood and youth, and even in manhood, as the humble, lowly son of the carpenter, could be the illustrious Son of David, and the glorious King, who was expected to deliver the people of Israel. How long this state of disbelief continued, we are unable to determine. Indeed we do not know that he became fully a disciple of the Lord, until after this interview, or that this was not the means employed by our Lord to cause his conversion. But as all the other persons to whom Jesus appeared after the resurrection were believers, and as the general belief of the early Christian writers is in favour of an earlier conversion, the probability is that he believed in the claims of our Lord before the crucifixion, and only needed such confirmation of his faith, and such correction of his views, as would be afforded by this interview.

After the day of pentecost, he occupied a most important position in the Christian church, and one for which his previous history peculiarly fitted him. He was the representative of the extreme Jewish element in the church. This appears from the fact that the judaizing disciples in Antioch, who caused Peter to dissemble, (Gal. 2. 12, 13,) are called "certain that came from James." That they pushed his principles too far, is almost certain, but the fact that they claimed James as their leader shows his position in this matter. As Paul represented the extreme Gentile ground, Peter an intermediate one, so

James seems to have been the representative of the extreme Jewish ground, and thus to have been qualified to act as a mediator between Jews and Christians. His strict observance of the Jewish law, and his almost ascetic purity of life, commanded for him the full confidence of the most bigoted Jews, whilst he had already that of the Christians. It was perhaps for this reason that he acted as the chief spokesman in the first synod, which declared that the observance of the Mosaic law was not obligatory on the Gentiles. His opinion would be of decisive weight with the judaizing part of the church. And it was in the same wise spirit of compromise that he advised Paul (Acts 21.20-25) to purify himself according to the law in the case of vows, in order that he might not offend the prejudices of the Jewish multitude. He was thus a transition link between the two dispensations, and presented to the Jews the best possible form of the Christian faith for their acceptance and approval. It was in special kindness to them that such a type of Christianity was presented to them, for by it their introduction to the truth in Jesus was made peculiarly easy. In James they saw that the most blameless reverence for Moses was no barrier to the reception of Christ, and if unable with such a type of Old Testament piety to receive New Testament truth, there remained no further possible means. Hence James did not itinerate, like the other apostles, as far as we can learn, but remained in Jerusalem, where he could most readily have access to the Jews. When he had laboured in person for some time, he sent forth the epistle that bears his name, "to the twelve tribes scattered abroad," (James 1.1,)* thus confirming the fact that his mission was one mainly to the Jews. Nor did his life continue beyond the period when the mission could be fulfilled. He is alleged to have been martyred nearly forty years after the erection of the Christian church, and shortly before the downfall of Jerusalem, after which event the Jews became generally so hostile to Christianity that but few conversions took place among them.

Hence his great work seems to have been to gather the elect remnant of the Jewish church into the Christian, and thus bring in "the children of the kingdom," and for this work it is plain that he was specially fitted in every respect.

It is here that we may find the meaning of this appearance. If James were then a disciple at all, it is probable that his faith before this time was clouded with Jewish prejudices. He did not see clearly the truth as it was in Jesus. It was therefore needful that our Lord should appear to him, and by confirming his faith in the most immovable manner, by enlarging his knowledge of the great plan of salvation, and by giving him such visions of the future as he needed, prepare him for the great work he was to do in the Christian church, and the self-denials and sufferings that were necessarily connected with that work. As the representative of the religion of Christ to the Jews, as the first pastor of the church in Jerusalem, the Moderator of the first General Synod of the church, the adviser and guide of Paul, and the writer of a canonical epistle, he needed both a firm faith and an intelligent one, and to give him both, our Lord granted him a special interview. Hence this personal and private appearance had the same general character with those to Peter, the men of Emmaus, and Thomas, and presents our Lord in the same beautiful light of condescension to infirmity, and kindness to imperfection that is exhibited in the others. The result was the same as in the other cases; this stern and high-hearted child of Abraham from that time never faltered in his confession of Christ, until he sealed that confession with his blood.

It is worthy of remark also, that the precise communications made at that time are not recorded in Scripture. The general reason is the same as in the previous cases. The main purpose of the interview was to terminate with James himself, and to affect others only in an indirect manner through him. Hence only the fact of its occurrence is mentioned. We would gladly in this case, and in the appearance to the five hundred, approach nearer the scene itself, and gaze on its wonderful sights, and listen to its wonderful words. But the Scripture never satisfies mere curiosity. It reveals just what is needful, and no more. Indeed its silence is often more significant than speech. There is a sublime reserve in regard to many things which proves its divine origin more fully than any words could do. There are many facts above and before us that to our present minds are as utterly incomprehensible as the Oberland Alps to a fish in the sea, and the very attempt to reveal them would indicate an ignorance and weakness that would disprove any divine origin in the book that made it. "It doth not yet appear what we shall be," and the things that Paul saw in paradise were "unutterable." Hence the silence of the Bible concerning these points, standing in such marked contrast with the detailed minuteness of all spurious revelations, is a striking proof that it is from that God, whose glory lies much more in what has not been revealed, than in what has; for the revealed is finite, whilst the unrevealed is infinite. The silence of Scripture in this case of James, is then only in accordance with a general law that stamps it as a revelation from God.

The general teaching of this appearance is substantially the same with some of the others, and hence need not be elaborated. It assures us that when God calls a man to a special work, he will give him special preparation; that when Jesus intends to use us for any peculiar service or suffering in the history of the church, he will give us such a manifestation of himself, as will fit us to do and to suffer his holy will; and that the very imperfections of human opinion and human character may be used in the work of redemption to accomplish ends that a more absolute perfection might fail to reach; and that the books that eternity shall open for our perusal contain the solution of many a mystery that has baffled us here on earth.

CHAPTER 15

THE TENTH APPEARANCE—THE APOSTOLIC COMMISSION IN MATTHEW

The place, Jerusalem and Olivet—The four forms of the commission—Why? —Their distinctness—Meaning of the commission—Not the original authority to preach and baptize. I. *Authority* of the commission. The mediatorial kingdom of Christ—All power. II. *The commission.* (1) To make disciples. (2) To baptize disciples—Subjects of baptism—Baptismal formula—Trinity. (3) To teach disciples—Inspiration—The three offices of Christ. III. *Encouragement.* The presence of Christ—I AM— "All days"—Days of worship, of toil, of trial, and of death.

> "O thou who mournest on thy way,
> With longings for the close of day,
> He walks with thee, that angel kind,
> And gently whispers, 'Be resigned;'
> Bear up—bear on—the end shall tell,
> The dear Lord ordereth all things well."

"And Jesus came and spake unto them, saying, All power is given unto me in heaven and in earth. Go ye therefore and teach all nations, baptizing them in the name of the Father, and of the Son, and of the Holy Ghost; teaching them to observe all things whatsoever I have commanded you, and lo! I am with you alway, even unto the end of the world. Amen."—Matt. 28.18-20.

We now reach the last, and in some respects the most important, appearance of our Lord to his disciples. The place of its occurrence was partly Jerusalem, and partly the mount of Olives. The probability is, that like the other appearances in Jerusalem, it was by night, and being the last interview that they were to have on earth, that it was prolonged through the entire night; and as the morning began to break over the eastern hills, that they went forth by that familiar path, so often trodden, across the Kedron, past Gethsemane, with its wondrous memories, up the Mount of Olives, whence the city could be seen, bathed in the light of the early morning, over the summit of the mount, until they reached that quiet and sheltered spot overhanging Bethany, whence he "ascended on high, leading captivity captive." If these conjectures be true, and they seem to be demanded by the different records of this last interview, there were many instructions given by our Lord that have not been recorded by the evangelists. Each one has recorded what was necessary for the purposes of his Gospel, and each one differs in some respects from the rest.

A neglect of these facts has led to some errors in the interpretation of the recorded words of the Gospels. Regarding them as perhaps but a single utterance of our Lord, it has been thought necessary to weave them into a continuous discourse, and thus make a harmony of them, an effort that does violence to some of the sentences in a most palpable manner. But if we remember that the interview was probably protracted through an entire night, that he appeared to them perhaps during their evening meal, and blessed and brake the bread before them, and continued for several hours to instruct them in the things pertaining to the kingdom, and prolonged these instructions during the long walk from the upper chamber to the scene of the ascension on the eastern slope of the Mount of Olives, we will see that very much must have been said by him, and that each evangelist must make only a selection for the particular purposes of his Gospel. Hence instead of attempting to make a harmony of these records, which usually makes a confusion of them, we prefer to take them just as they are given; believing that there was a reason for the variations, which requires that each record should be considered apart from the others, and not in forced amalgamation with them as is commonly done.

The ultimate reasons for the different forms in which we

find the apostolic commission recorded, will probably be found to coincide with the ultimate reasons for the different Gospels in which they are written. What these reasons are must be left in some measure, to conjecture. That there were satisfactory reasons requiring that the life of our Lord should be recorded in four Gospels, instead of one, must be conceded by all, and probably the same reasons required four records of the apostolic commission. There are some facts that present themselves to us very clearly in regard to these Gospels. The general impression of the church has always been, that Matthew wrote for the Hebrews, Mark for the Latins, and Luke for the Greeks, whilst John wrote with a wider immediate scope, and at a later date, and hence presented the final facts that were needed to supplement the rest. There seems to be no good reason for setting aside these opinions. The Hebrews, Romans, and Greeks were the three great representative nations of that day, and embodied the ideas of theology, law, and literature, in which they were then severally pre-eminent, each in its peculiar department. Through the Hebrew people, we have received all that is most valuable to us in religious truth; through the Romans, all that is most permanent in political organization and legal forms; and through the Greeks, all that is consummate in literature, philosophy, and art. It was but a shadowing forth of these facts that was presented in the inscription on the cross, that was written in the Hebrew, Latin, and Greek, the languages of these representative peoples. But there was a fourth kingdom then set up, the kingdom of the Incarnate Word, and the dispensation of the Holy Ghost; and the great peculiarities of this kingdom are presented in their deepest forms in the fourth Gospel by John, whilst the paramount agency of the Spirit is acknowledged in the fourth form of the commission as it is recorded in the Acts of the Apostles, a book that has sometimes been called the Gospel of the Holy Ghost.

We find in each of the four records the precise peculiarities that mark the Gospel in which it is found. The commission in Matthew presents the mediatorial dominion of Christ, the divinity of Jesus, the Trinity, the organic unity and functions of the church, and the doctrine of baptism; all which great religious ideas were needful to be presented to the Hebrew mind, as we learn from their elaborate presentation in the Epistle to the Hebrews. The commission in Mark is brief, terse, and sententious, like a decree of the Roman Senate, and uses the word gospel, and presents the great doctrine of justification by faith, which we find so fully set forth in the Epistle to the Romans. The forms in Luke and the Acts in like manner, as will be more fully shown hereafter, present precisely the doctrines and facts that we would infer from the apparent design of each book. Hence to fuse these different promulgations of the commission into a single continuous statement is to lose their peculiar significance, and defeat the purpose of the record.

Another preliminary question demands our consideration. What was the precise purpose of the apostolic commission? The opinion that is very prevalently held, is, that it conveyed the original authority of the apostles to preach and baptize, and hence contains the full and authoritative statement of the subjects and limitations of both these duties of their office. But a little reflection will show the error of this view. The ordination and consequent authority to preach and baptize had been given long before, but restricted to the Jews, and restricted as to the fulness of the truth presented. The record of this transaction will be found in the three evangelists, Matthew 10.1-23; Mark 3.13-19; and Luke 6.13-16. In these passages it is stated that he "ordained twelve that they should be with him, and that he might send them forth to preach," (Mark 3.14,) and that he forbade them to preach to the Gentiles and Samaritans, requiring them to go only "to the lost sheep of the house of Israel," (Matt. 10.5, 6.) That they also baptized is evident from John 3.22-26; and 4.1, 2, where it is expressly stated, in reference to a very early period of our Lord's ministry, that his disciples baptized. Hence the authority to baptize must have been conferred with the authority to preach, and have had the same restrictions to the house of Israel. Both the preaching and baptism had reference to the new form of dispensation that was to be given to the church, and both were restricted to the Jews until that dispensation was fully ushered in. Here was the original ordination of the apostles, and their commission to preach, and baptize, and their authority dates from this point, and not from this last interview of our Lord.

What then was the purport of this apostolic commission, so called, that was given at this final interview? It was simply the authority to do that to all nations, which they had hitherto been directed to confine to the Jews, and the announcement of the final and perfect form of the kingdom of heaven, as a way of salvation for sinners. They had preached to and baptized only the Jews hitherto, now they were to preach to and baptize all nations.

This will be unanswerably evident from a simple comparison of the four forms of the commission. Had they been the original authority to preach and baptize, we would find this included in each form of the commission; but the facts are that two of them omit all reference to baptism at all, and the only point in which they all agree is the one mentioned, that this commission previously given was now extended from one nation to all nations. To exhibit this we present the four forms together for comparison, italicising the only thing common to all.

Matthew 28.18-20.—"All power is given unto me in heaven and in earth. Go ye, therefore, and teach *all nations*, baptizing them in the name of the Father, and of the Son, and of the Holy Ghost; teaching them to observe all things whatsoever I have commanded you, and lo! I am with you alway, even to the end of the world. Amen."

Mark 16.15-18.—"And he said unto them, Go ye into *all the world*, and preach the gospel to *every creature*. He that believeth and is baptized shall be saved; but he that believeth not shall be damned. And these signs shall follow them that believe: In my name shall they cast out devils; they shall speak with new tongues; they shall take up serpents; and if they drink any deadly thing, it shall not hurt them; they shall lay hands on the sick, and they shall recover."

Luke 24.44-49.—"And he said unto them, These are the words which I spake unto you, while I was yet with you, that all things must be fulfilled which were written in the law of Moses, and in the prophets, and in the psalms, concerning me. Then opened he their understanding, that they might understand the scriptures, and said unto them, Thus it is written, and thus it behoved Christ to suffer, and to rise from the dead the third day: and that repentance and remission of sins should be preached in his name among *all nations*, beginning at Jerusalem. And ye are witnesses of these things. And, behold, I send the promise of my Father upon you: but tarry ye in the city of Jerusalem, until ye be endued with power from on high."

Acts 1.4-8—And being assembled together with them, commanded them that they should not depart from Jerusalem, but wait for the promise of the Father, which, saith he, ye have heard of me: for John truly baptized with water; but ye shall be baptized with the Holy Ghost not many days hence. When they therefore were come together, they asked of him, saying, Lord, wilt thou at this time restore again the kingdom to Israel? And he said unto them, It is not for you to know the times or the seasons which the Father hath put in his own power. But ye shall receive power after that the Holy Ghost is come upon you: and ye shall be witnesses unto me both in Jerusalem, and in all Judea, and in Samaria, and unto the *uttermost part of the earth*."

Here it will be seen that the only point common to all these forms is that of extension to all nations, showing that this was the essential fact in the commission, and that it was not the primary grant to preach and baptize, but a simple extension of the authority to perform these acts, before given and restricted to one nation, now to be carried to all nations, because the church with which these functions were connected was now to be extended in the same manner.

We are now prepared to consider the form of the commission given us in the Gospel of Matthew, where we have the authority of the commission. the commission itself, and the encouragements given to those who were to execute it.

1. *The authority of the commission.* "All power is given unto me in heaven and in earth."

The word here rendered power* means strictly authority, or the right to exercise power. Hence it is not omnipotence that our Lord here claims for himself. This power, he says, was "given" to him, which could not be said of omnipotence, for that is incommunicable, and could not have been given to any finite being; and moreover belonged to him by nature, so that it was not needful that it should have been given.

The power or authority here referred to is that which was bestowed upon him as Mediator, for the purpose of executing the great plan of redemption. The divine nature of the Son had no beginning, being eternal; but that mysterious personality, in which the divine and human natures were united in the Mediatorial person, the God-man, this had a beginning, and was capable of receiving grants of authority. That such a grant was made appears not only from this statement, but from the memorable passage in Philippians, (c. 2.5-11.) It is there stated that as a reward of the sufferings of Jesus, God exalted him and gave him a name—*i.e.*, an authority, or office—above every name, that at the name of Jesus every knee should bow, and every tongue acknowledge him Lord.

---

*Exousia

Here is a specific grant of official authority as a consequence of his sufferings, that is obviously the same referred to by our Lord in this declaration in Matthew. It is a delegated king-ship over the universe, which is granted to him as Mediator, for the purpose of subduing the rebellion of sin, and which he will hold until that rebellion is subdued, when he will deliver it up again to the Father. This is the express assurance of Scripture. After the resurrection and final judgment, "Then cometh the end, when he shall have delivered up the kingdom to God, even the Father, when he shall have put down all rule, and all authority, and power. And when all things shall be subdued unto him, then shall the Son also himself be sub-ject unto him that put all things under him, that God may be all in all." 1 Cor. 15.24-28.

Here we have announced to us the sublime fact, that the universe is now under the Mediatorial dominion of Jesus, for the purpose of subduing sin. That great revolt, which began in heaven and was transferred to earth, is to be put down by the Son. For this purpose he assumed human nature, and became a new and wonderful Person—a Person capable of suffering and obeying, by virtue of its human element, and of atoning and reigning, by virtue of its Divine: and to this Per-son is delegated the rule of the universe until the economy of redemption is completed. Heaven, earth, and hell, are all put in subjection to him, that he may redeem men on earth, and saving them from hell exalt them to heaven, and thus bring the universe back to more than its former allegiance. Hence the economy of God's government now is not what it was before sin entered, or what it will be after the mystery of redemption is finished, under the rule of the Father alone. It is under the Mediatorial regency of the Immanuel, the God-man Mediator, and will be so until the mighty plan of redemption is completed. Hence is it that in heaven angels and redeemed ones behold and worship "a Lamb slain, in the midst of the throne;" and that from hell, the very devils beseech him that they may not be tormented before the time. And hence is it that the sublime assurance is given by Paul to the Christian, "All things are yours, whether Paul, or Apollos, or Cephas, or the world, or life, or death, or things present, or things to come, all are yours, for ye are Christ's, and Christ is God's." 1 Cor. 3.21-23. Hence we have the great fact laid down, as the basis of all ministerial authority, that the world belongs to Jesus; it has been granted to him as Mediator, and all men are bound to acknowledge him in this character, and bow to his kingly authority. All agencies, natural and supernatural, are placed in his hand to secure this ultimate recognition. All powers are subordinated to him, so that he has not only the right to command the obedience of all men, but also the power to secure that obedience in whatever way he may deem best. This kingly authority then is the real and fitting ground on which the commission is rested, by which the apostles were to go forth and summon the submission of all nations.

2. *The commission itself.* Go ye therefore, and teach all nations, baptizing them in the name of the Father, and of the Son, and of the Holy Ghost; teaching them to observe all things whatsoever I have commanded you."

The general purport of this commission has been already explained. The church was now to be extended to all nations, and hence the right to preach and baptize, before restricted to the Jews, was now extended to all the world. The commission includes three particulars. They were to go forth among all nations, and (1) *make disciples*, (2) *baptize the disciples* thus made, and (3) *teach the disciples* thus baptized the whole counsel of God, as revealed by our Lord Jesus Christ.

(1) *They were to make disciples from all nations.* The word here rendered "teach" means literally, and properly, to "make disciples," and is distinct from the word "teach." The precise idea conveyed in it is expressed fully in John 4.1, "The Pharisees had heard that Jesus made and baptized more disci-

ples than John." Here to make disciples is obviously not to teach them, but simply to cause them in some way publicly to enroll themselves as his disciples, and in consequence of that discipleship to be baptized. In the commission, this making disciples and baptizing, before limited to the Jews, was extended to all nations. The teaching was to come after they had been made disciples. To render this word by teaching alone, is to make our Lord command the disciples to go and teach all nations, teaching them, a tautology that ought not to be charged on his words. Hence the true meaning of the word is *making disciples.* *

How they are to be made disciples must of course depend on the character of the persons themselves. The great fact is that they are to be made disciples, brought into the relation of professed and acknowledged learners from the great Teacher, and led to him as the only way of access to God. Christ stands at the threshold of the kingdom of God, and must be acknowledged before an entrance can be made to its inner blessings. In this acknowledgment we have a recognition of the prophetic office of Christ, when we come and cleave to him as disciples, to learn the will of God for our salvation.

(2) *They were to baptize the disciples thus made.* It is impossible for us to gather any full account of either the nature or subjects of baptism from this commission. It was not the design of our Lord to do this, nor was it necessary, as

---

*That this meaning of the word is not adopted from any doctrinal preferences, will appear from the fact that it is preferred by critics who cannot be suspected of any such preferences. Kuinoël, who is surely safe from any such suspicion, says, on v. 19, *"matheteuein* is not to teach, for it is clearly distinguished from *didaskein* v. 20, and they who by baptism were received into the company of Christians, were afterwards more accurately instructed. It simply denotes "to make a disciple, to receive into the company of Christians." Bengel makes the same distinction, *"matheteuein* is to make disciples, and embraces baptism and teaching." Other testimonies equally explicit could readily be given from Olshausen, Stier, and others.

they had already no doubt received full information on these points when they were first ordained. The law here announced is that all who are made disciples are to be baptized. The question as to the proper subjects of baptism is simply, Who are capable of being made disciples? Can any be constituted disciples by birth, and entered into the school of Christ by the act of their parents? Is the kingdom of Christ only a school for the adult disciple, or is it also a training institute for the youthful disciple? We believe, that like the family, and the state, it was designed by God to be an educational institute for the young, as well as for the old, and that this is one of its most precious features. The lambs are entrusted to the shepherd as well as the sheep, and belong to the flock as truly as they do. So the children of believing parents are made disciples as truly as the parents themselves, and as such have a right to the same ordinance of recognition and initiation.

The baptismal formula is one of the deepest significance. It is required that the disciples of Jesus shall be baptized *into* the name of the Father, Son, and Holy Ghost. What is the meaning of this? It is not merely by their authority, for the words indicate much more than that. The meaning of the phrase, is, that by the baptism there is signed and sealed a close and vital relation to the Father, Son, and Holy Ghost, each of whom performs a part in the work of salvation. The outward application of water is a symbol of purification from sin, and this being done into the name of the Trinity, it is thus declared that each Person of that mysterious nature bears a part in this great work of salvation, and that the person baptized is brought into a relation of the deepest obligation to them all. Baptism is then a public avowal that the person baptized is devoted to the Triune God through the atoning work of Jesus Christ, who, as the great High Priest, has made a perfect sacrifice, and thus opened a way of access to God.

The baptismal formula is an assertion of the doctrine of the Trinity that no ingenuity can set aside. It is very certain that the Father is a Person, and the Son a Person, and hence it must follow that the Holy Ghost also is a Person, and thus we have three Persons presented to us. But these three are in another sense one, for but one Name is ascribed to them. If they were distinct natures as well as distinct Persons, baptism would have been in their names, and not their Name. But there is ascribed to the three only a single Name, which here, as elsewhere, denotes the essence of the Being to whom it is attached. This fact proves that whilst in Personal distinctions they are Three, so that Personal names and actions may be ascribed to each, yet in essence and nature they are one, so that but a single Name can be rightly ascribed to this mysterious and adorable Nature. Hence we have here the proclamation of the ineffable Name of that great Being, who appeared to the Patriarchs as the Almighty God, the Elohim; to the chosen seed, as Jehovah, the I AM of his own people; but to those who live under the third great dispensation of the covenant, as the Father, Son, and Holy Ghost, three Persons, but one God—three Persons, the same in substance, but equal in power and glory. This, however, is the doctrine of the Trinity.

(3) *They were to teach the disciples thus baptized, all that Jesus commanded them.* "Teaching them to observe all things whatsoever I have commanded you."

These words imply a promise of plenary inspiration, for they constitute the apostles the vehicles through which the commands of Jesus are to be transmitted to us. Now as these commands are to be kept on pain of the most fearful condemnation, we cannot conceive it possible that our Lord would not secure a transmission of them that would be infallible. To ordain a law, the violation of which involves the severest penalty, and yet make no provision for the certain and infallible record of that law, would be a refinement of cruelty that can never be charged on the kingdom of Christ. Hence we have here a formal investiture of the apostles with that high function of conveying Christ's words to the world in speech and writing, from which we have the inspired Scriptures of the New Testament.

We have in the three clauses of the apostolic commission a recognition of the three offices which Christ executes as our Redeemer. When men are "made disciples," there is recognized his Prophetic office, by which he is the great Teacher of the will of God for the salvation of men. When they are "baptized as disciples," unto remission of sins, there is a recognition of his Priestly office, by which this remission is purchased and applied, and through which the gift of the sanctifying Spirit was procured and sent into the world. When they are "taught as disciples," to observe all the commands of Christ, there is an acknowledgment of his Kingly office, by virtue of which he has the right to command, and we are bound to obey all that he has thus commanded. Thus Christ is set forth in all the wondrous and manifold riches of his character and offices, as the great subject of gospel preaching, the great object of gospel faith, and the great end of gospel obedience. Men in their ignorance must be led to him to know the way of approach to God; in their guilt, to receive forgiveness and acceptance; and in their weakness to receive strength and guidance; so that Christ must be to them the Alpha and Omega, the centre and circumference of a complete and full-orbed piety.

3. *We have the encouragement given to those who are to execute this commission.* "Lo! I am with you alway, even unto the end of the world."

The encouragement is the perpetual presence of Christ. We are prone to think of Jesus as a being of eighteen hundred years ago, or at least as a resident in heaven, and to attach the idea of distance and separation to him. This prevents us from feeling his influence with that real and living power that ought to accompany it. When we think of one as dead or distant, we cease to feel his personal power as we do when we think of him as near and living. Hence it is that our Lord assures us that he is neither dead nor distant, but near us, with us, and with us at all times and places of the future.

There are two peculiarities of expression here that deserve notice. The first is the mode in which he speaks of his presence. He does not say, *I will be* with you always, but *I am* with you, developing thus the fact that he spake as the Divine Redeemer, that eternal and self-existent Being, to whom there is neither future nor past, but one unchanging, eternal NOW. The promise to be with them always to the end of the world, implies that it was not addressed to them as individuals merely, but as representatives of the church, for *they* were not to live always, to the end of the world. This proves at once the perpetuity of the church, and the divinity of the Saviour. If he is to be with his church to the end of the world, the church shall exist to that time, and hence be perpetual. If he is to be with his people scattered through all ages and lands, at all times, he must be omnipresent, and therefore divine. Hence we have two implied claims of attributes belonging to God alone in these words, proving that he who uttered them was the Incarnate Word, "God manifest in the flesh," "God over all, blessed for ever."

The second peculiarity of phrase here is the words rendered "alway," which are literally "all the days," not merely always, but all kinds of days, that were before them—days of light and of shadow, sunshine and storm, heat and cold, all the varying days of their destiny his presence should be with them; a pillar of cloud, when the heat and burden of the day came pouring down in a pressure of toil and sorrow; a pillar of fire, when cloud and darkness gathered over the path, giving cheer and guidance when all other lights had gone out; the shadow of a great rock in a weary land, when the sun beat fiercely on their heads; and a covert from the tempest, "when the blast of the terrible ones is a storm against the wall."

But what is the nature of this presence? It is not simply the presence of the Holy Spirit, for he says expressly "*I*" will be with you, announcing a Personal presence with his ministers and people, of a real and most important character. It is not the presence of his human nature, for that is in heaven, and has not been invested with divine attributes, as it must be, were it present at all times and places. It is then the presence in a peculiar and precious sense of his divine nature, just as he has promised it in the words, "Where two or three are gathered together in my name, there am I in the midst of them" Matt. 18.20; and just as it is realized in the ordinances and especially the sacraments of the church, and the lives of God's people.

The promise then is one of unspeakable richness and comfort. Christ will be with us through "all days," and as our day our strength shall be. Is it a day of *worship?* He will be in the midst of the two or three who are gathered in the little prayer-meeting, as well as with the great congregation, in which a thousand voices swell the song of praise, and a thousand hearts respond to the words of prayer. He will also be with the lonely worshipper who enters into his closet, and with a burdened heart and a quivering lip prays to his Father which is in secret. He will be with the little company that gather with tearful eyes around the communion table, and will whisper to them, "Fear not, little flock, for it is your Father's good pleasure to give you the kingdom." He will be with the drooping minister, as he stands up with a faltering heart to proclaim the Word of God under discouragement, and will whisper to him as he did to the disheartened Paul in Corinth, "Be not afraid, but speak, and hold not thy peace, *for I am with thee,* and no man shall set on thee to hurt thee, for I have much people in this city." Acts 18.9, 10. But for this sweet promise many a heart would have sunk in attempting to preach the gospel to others.

Is it a day of *toil?* The work to which they were summoned was one of amazing, indeed of appalling magnitude. It was the conversion of the world to God, the downfall of all that was strongest and dearest to Jew and Gentile, and the establishment of a religion of self-denial and toil. Well might they shrink from a work so vast, but for this promise, which secured more to be with them than were against them, and enabled them to wield a power that was mighty to the pulling down of strong holds. We are not therefore surprised that before the last of that company on Olivet was called home, the gospel had been preached to the very ends of the earth. But the same cheering presence is needed still, for the work is still a vast, and almost an appalling one. Nor less deeply is it needed in every work of the Christian life. We can "do all things," only when Christ strengthens us with his presence. With that presence we need not falter, for he is mighty to save, and will give us the victory at last over every opposition.

Is it a day of *trial?* Many a child of God has had these days, but many a one has also had the presence of Jesus to support in them. They have had trials of cruel mockings, and scourgings, and every form of suffering, and yet been sustained through them all by the hope of a better country. In poverty Jesus has told them of the heavenly riches; in sickness, of the land where the inhabitant no more says, "I am sick;" in loneliness, of a presence closer than that of the dearest on earth; in danger, of a succour that no human power could break down. As Paul stood before Nero, or lay in the Mamertine prison, he tells the secret of his unquailing courage, "The Lord stood with me and strengthened me." As others have entered the furnace, and felt the flame kindling upon them, the fourth form of the Babylonian furnace has been beside them, and delivered them from the very smell of fire. In the catacombs of Rome, among the crags of Piedmont, along the plains of France, through the glens of Scotland, and wherever a martyred disciple has borne high testimony for Jesus, there has he been beside the sufferer to fulfil his promise. And with the widowed, the orphaned, the neglected and pining ones, whom all others have forsaken, there has been ever this abiding presence, that enabled them to feel that the sufferings of this present time are not worthy to be compared with the glory that shall be revealed to us.

Is it the day of *death?* Even there, and even more fully there, has this promise been verified in the past, and shall be in the future. In that lonely valley, Jesus has always met his trusting and obedient ones, and his rod and staff have sustained them there. Stephen found him there as he cried, "Lord Jesus, receive my spirit," and Paul found him there, as he exultingly looked up to the crown of righteousness, when the time of his departure was at hand. Thus has it been, and thus shall it be, for when heart and flesh shall fail, he shall be the strength of our heart; and as we go down into the dark valley, his presence shall make the valley all light.

CHAPTER 16

THE TENTH APPEARANCE—APOSTOLIC COMMISSION IN MARK

The difference between Matthew and Mark, just such as we would expect—The Roman gospel. I. *The commission.* Its extent—Are infants excluded from baptism by its terms?—The illogical inference—Why infants are not named in the commission—The real warrant of the commission. II. *The authenticating seals.* The miracles of the soul. III. *The consequences of accepting or rejecting*—The awful words—Eternity the only interpreter.

> " 'Go preach my gospel,' saith the Lord,
> 'Bid the whole earth my grace receive;
> He shall be saved who trusts my word;
> He shall be damned that won't believe.
> I'll make your great commission known,
> And ye shall prove my gospel true,
> By all the works that I have done,
> By all the wonders ye shall do.' "

"And he said unto them, Go ye into all the world, and preach the gospel to every creature. He that believeth and is baptized shall be saved; but he that believeth not shall be damned. And these signs shall follow them that believe: In my name shall they cast out devils; they shall speak with new tongues; they shall take up serpents; and if they drink any deadly thing, it shall not hurt them; they shall lay hands on the sick, and they shall recover." Mark 16.15—18.

The narrative of Mark is condensed, and hence sometimes difficult to adjust to the other Gospels. The apostolic commission, as he gives it, is closely connected on the one hand with the appearance to the eleven, as they sat at meat, in v. 14, and on the other with the ascension in vs. 19, 20. As those two facts were certainly separated by an interval of some days, or

weeks, it is obvious that the evangelist did not intend to give
these events in reference to their exact chronology, but only
in reference to their general connection. Hence we may, without the least violence, connect the commission with the events
of vs. 19, 20, rather than with those of v. 14, since it must be
disconnected with one or the other as to the precise time of its
utterance. This then will place it, where it certainly belongs,
in the tenth appearance of our Lord in Jerusalem and upon
Olivet, in connection with his ascension. It is true that we
might refer the appearance in v. 14 to this last occasion, and
suppose that it described the last interview which began in
the city and ended on the Mount of Olives, but the general
judgment of expositors and the most natural conclusion is,
that it refers to one or two appearances soon after the resurrection, recorded by the other evangelists.

The form of the commission in Mark differs from that in
Matthew, precisely as the Gospels differ, and precisely as we
would expect them to differ from the general design of the
two Gospels. Matthew, writing for the Hebrews, presents the
doctrines that were most important for them, as we gather
from the epistle to the Hebrews, and brings out the connection between the Old and New Testament church, the divinity of Christ, the Trinity, and the perpetuity of the church.
Mark, writing for the Roman world, brings out the very doctrines most important for them, as we learn from the epistle
to the Romans. The very word "gospel," which is the text of
the epistle to the Romans, (Rom. 1.16,) occurs only in this
form of the commission, and the great doctrine of justification by faith, which is the substance of that epistle, is also the
substance of this form of the commission. The authenticating
seals promised in this commission are precisely those that
would most readily strike the practical intellect of the
Romans and Gentiles generally, and did in fact do so, as we
learn from the history of the church. Hence we see how
admirably adapted was this selection from the ample utter-

ances of our Lord on this occasion, for the purposes of Mark.

We have here, 1. The commission; 2. The seals authenticating it; 3. The consequences of accepting or rejecting it.

1. *The Commission itself.* "Go ye into all the world, and preach the gospel to every creature. He that believeth and is baptized shall be saved, but he that believeth not shall be damned."

We here perceive again the fact that this was not the original ordination to preach and baptize, but only an extension of the right to do so, from one nation to the whole world. The original ordination is mentioned by Mark in ch. 3.14-19. In ch. 1.14, 15, he tells us that Jesus came into Galilee preaching the gospel and calling on men to repent and believe the gospel. In ch. 3.14-19, he informs us that our Lord ordained the twelve to go and preach this gospal, omitting the fact mentioned by Matthew, in writing for the Hebrews, that they were restricted in this preaching (and of course in the baptism that we learn from John 4.1, 2, was connected with it) to the house of Israel. Now when the kingdom was fully come, and the gospel complete, they were sent to proclaim it to all nations, and baptize all who would accept it.

It is therefore wholly illogical to infer that this passage is final and exclusive in regard to the subject of baptism. As this inference is pressed by many, we cannot pass it by without some remark.

The argument is, Christ says nothing in this passage about infant baptism, though he was speaking on the subject of baptism. We reply, he says nothing about infant salvation, though he was speaking on the subject of salvation. Hence the inference that excludes them by this passage from baptism, also excludes them from salvation. Indeed it is stronger in the latter case than the former, because of the reverse form of the proposition. In the first clause it is not said that one who does not believe shall not be baptized, but in the second clause, it is expressly said that one who does not believe shall not be saved. Hence if this passage excludes infants from baptism, much more does it exclude them from salvation. If we recoil from this inference, and say that the passage only refers to those capable of faith, to adults, then if this is true as to salvation, it is equally true as to baptism, and hence it cannot be fairly used as an argument against the baptism of infants.

If it be asked, Why did our Lord not designate all the subjects of baptism? we reply that he was not explaining the condition of baptism, but of salvation. Hence though he names baptism in the first clause, he omits it in the second, and Luke in recording the words omits it from both. If it be further asked why he did not explain who were to be the proper subjects of baptism, we reply, because this explanation had no doubt been given when the original commission to teach and baptize was granted three years before; and it was just as needless to explain the proper subject of baptism, as of ordination to the ministry, or admission to the Lord's Supper, or any other question of church order and government, already explained.

The simple purport of the commission was that having hitherto preached to and baptized Jews only, they must now preach to and baptize all nations, as the great redemption, indicated by this preparatory preaching and baptism, was now finished. That this commission involved no restriction of baptism to adults may be illustrated by a simple supposition. Suppose that instead of baptism it had been circumcision that was enjoined, and the statement had been "he that believeth and is circumcised shall be saved," would any one have dreamed that infants were thereby excluded from circumcision? If not from circumcision, then they could not be from baptism, by these words.

The apostolic commission is a simple warrant to extend that church to all nations, that had hitherto been confined to one nation. Hence no explanation of the law of membership in that church was needed, unless some change was ordained.

That law, which embodied infant membership, had been in existence for two thousand years, and become familiar as a household word. It was not needed to explain that law any more than the law of praise, prayer, or the Sabbath. When the church was thus extended, the law of membership went with it, unless repealed. As the New Testament is silent about any such repeal, it follows that the law of membership is unchanged, and that the promise is still not only to us, but also to our children, and that Abraham is now the father of all them who believe, even though they are not circumcised.

The commission is therefore not only the warrant, but the command to engage in the work of missions. It is what Wellington called "the marching orders of the church," and indifference or neglect of missionary labour is disobedience of orders, and violation of the sacramental oath.

2. *The Seals authenticating the commission.*

These were to be miracles of five kinds, vs. 17, 18. The Book of Acts records the occurrence of all these miracles but one, which no doubt was wrought, though not recorded. The first miracle-seal was the casting out of demons, which took place at Philippi, when the spirit of divination was cast out of the damsel by Paul; and at Ephesus, when handkerchiefs, blessed by Paul, exorcised those possessed of devils, Acts 16.18; 19.12. The second was speaking with new tongues, which took place at pentecost, at the baptism of Cornelius, and at Corinth, as we learn from 1 Cor. 12.14. The third was taking up serpents without harm, which was done by Paul in Melita, Acts 28.3-6, and convinced the Maltese that he was more than an ordinary man, and his religion from God. The fourth was drinking any deadly poison with impunity, which no doubt happened, though it is not recorded. The fifth was laying hands on the sick for their recovery, which was done repeatedly by Paul, and by many others, as we learn from James 5.14, 15.

The seals were necessary to authenticate the apostolic

office, and hence continued as long as the office itself. When neither the office nor the seals were required by the state of the church, they both ceased, and miraculous powers were gradually withdrawn. Christianity is now itself the great standing miracle of the world, and its mighty works are not physical and bodily, but moral and spiritual. It still casts out demons, and has taken a John Newton, a Colonel Gardiner, or a savage Africaner, and transformed them into pure, gentle, and loving saints. There are thousands on earth, as well as in heaven, who need nothing more than their own experience to prove that the gospel still retains its ancient power of casting demons out of the soul. It still enables the Christian to speak with new tongues, putting a new song into his mouth, and enabling the lips that once were all dumb, to utter the language of Zion. There are still serpents that it enables one to take up harmlessly, the hissing brood of malice, envy, and calumny, which soon drop from the hand of innocence, leaving it unhurt. It still shields from the deadly cup of temptation and neutralizes its poisonous power, so that, if led into temptation, it at least delivers from evil. It still heals sickness, not of the body it is true, but of the soul, and whispers sweet hopes of the land where no one says, "I am sick." Hence its triumphs, if not so palpable to the senses as these literal miracles, are still authenticating seals of its divine warrant, for nothing could accomplish such works as these, unless it came from God.

3. *The Consequences of accepting or rejecting the proffer contained in this commission.*

These consequences are embodied in two of the most momentous words ever uttered by human lips, *salvation* and *damnation.* The meaning of these awful words it will require an eternity of experience to unfold. They involve all that is most joyous in heaven, and all that is most fearful in hell, for ever! When the great apostle had caught but a single glimpse of what is included in salvation, he came back saying that it was not only unlawful to utter the things that he saw, but impossible, for they were unutterable. And if the splendours of the heavenly city are thus unutterable, how much more the terrors of the dark region below! The very dimness and vagueness of the terms employed to describe its torments, are more terrible than the minutest description of details, for it tells us that they baffle description, and are unutterable.

That this should be hinged on simple faith or its absence seems strange, until we remember that man is lost already, a doomed rebel, a serpent-bitten wanderer in the desert, a shipwrecked mariner drowning in the sea. Pardon is offered to the rebel, healing to the dying wanderer, an ark of safety to the perishing voyager. To believe and accept is to be saved; to refuse or neglect is to allow the avenger of blood to come, the poison to do its fatal work, and the drowning one to perish in the waters, for "how shall we escape, if we neglect so great salvation?"

CHAPTER 17

THE TENTH APPEARANCE—APOSTOLIC COMMISSION IN LUKE

Differences between Luke and the other evangelists—The Greek gospel. I. *The Holy Scripture the only final and unerring rule of faith and practice.* Popery and infidelity—Jesus endorsing the Scripture. II. *The central doctrine of revelation, an atoning and suffering Messiah.* The law, prophets, and psalms—The cross of Christ the centre of all human history. III. *A divine power needful to enable man to comprehend the gospel of Christ.* "Opening the understanding"—The new light. IV. *The salvation of the gospel for all, however remote their habitation, or great their guilt.* "All nations"—"Beginning at Jerusalem"—Bunyan's Jerusalem sinner.

> "Thy glory O'er creation shines;
>   But in thy sacred Word,
> I read in fairer, brighter lines,
>   My bleeding, dying Lord."

"And he said unto them, These are the words which I spake unto you, while I was yet with you, that all things must be fulfilled which were written in the law of Moses, and in the prophets, and in the psalms, concerning me. Then opened he their understanding, that they might understand the scriptures, and said unto them, Thus it is written, and thus it behoved Christ to suffer, and to rise from the dead the third day: and that repentance and remission of sins should be preached in his name among all nations, beginning at Jerusalem. And ye are witnesses of these things." Luke 24.44-48.

In discussing the apostolic commission as it is given by the first two evangelists, we have seen how exactly the form of it was determined by the purpose of each Gospel. The evangelist Matthew, writing for the Hebrews, gives that portion of our Lord's instructions during that last memorable night and morning, which was most needful for the Hebrews, as we learn from the prominence given to them in the Epistle to the Hebrews. Mark, writing for the Roman world, presents the doctrines required by the Latin mind, as we gather from the stress laid on these doctrines in the epistle to the Romans. But Luke addressed a yet different audience, the third representative people of the ancient world, the great Grecian race, that was scattered so widely over the earth, and played so important a part in history. They were polished with intellectual culture, and had a vast literature of their own, and a language so widely diffused that it was the best possible vehicle for a revelation that was designed for the whole world. Hence Luke adopts a more strict historical method, and bases his Gospel more on existing records, and gives prominence to the Scriptures. Whilst Matthew made prominent the divinity of Christ, his mediatorial kingdom, and the Trinity; and Mark, the doctrine of justification by faith; Luke presents the authority of the holy Scripture, the doctrine of an atoning Messiah, and the need of divine illumination to understand the Scriptures. These were the doctrines needful to be made prominent to the Greeks, to whom they were foolishness. And it is a striking proof of the position already argued that the apostolic commission was not the original authority to baptize, that we find no mention made of baptism at all by Luke in his form of the commission. This can be explained only on the supposition that the authority had previously been granted, and hence it was not deemed necessary to repeat the grant here. The only point that it has in common with the other forms of the commission is, the extension of the grant to all nations that had hitherto been limited to the Jewish nation. There are several points of great importance presented in this form of the commission.

1. *The Holy Scripture is the only unerring and final rule of faith and practice.*

This is the great question of the day in which we live. Infidelity on one hand assails the sufficiency of Scripture, and presents human reason in one form as its supplement. Popery on the other hand assails it, and presents human reason in another form for the same purpose. Both agree in rejecting the Scripture as a final and sufficient rule, and in presenting human reason to correct it. They differ in the precise form in which we are to look for that reason: Infidelity contending for the cultivated reason of the present, Popery for the traditional reason of the past.

Against all these impugners we have the direct and thrice uttered recognition of Christ. He appeals to the fact that when he was with them, he told them "that all things must be fulfilled which were written in the law of Moses, and in the prophets, and in the psalms, concerning" him; he "opened their understanding that they might understand the scriptures," "and said unto them, Thus it is written, &c," giving by these three distinct recognitions of the binding authority of Scripture, the strongest proof of his views on this point. He makes no distinction as to portions of higher or lower authority, but places the entire Scripture on the commanding elevation of a supreme and divinely inspired rule of faith and practice, and one whose sufficiency was such as to need no supplementing authority or interpreter. Nor is his recognition limited to the portions of Scripture then written. The unwritten parts are equally endorsed in the words, "ye are witnesses of these things." v. 48. Here they were appointed to be the authorized witnesses of his gospel, and of course had assured to them the same reliable accuracy in delivering their testimony that he alleged in regard to the Old Testament witnesses, which was equivalent to a promise of inspiration. Hence we have here the great doctrine of the sufficiency of Scripture as a rule of faith and practice, that the church of God rests on the Bible, as its basis, and that all Scripture is given by inspiration of God, and is profitable for our instruction in what is needful to salvation.

2. *The great central doctrine of Revelation is a suffering and atoning Messiah.*

When Jesus comes to explain what is written concerning him in the Scripture, we find that it is, "thus it behoved Christ to suffer, and to rise from the dead the third day." v. 46. This was the great doctrine which to the Jews was a stumbling block, and to the Greeks, foolishness; and yet a doctrine taught in all the history, the revelation, and the types of the past, from Abel to John the Baptist.

The *law* spake of a suffering and atoning Messiah. Sacrifice would have been else an unmeaning cruelty. Every lamb, from that of Abel to Abraham, and the paschal lamb of Egypt, and the sacrificial pomp of Sinai, down to the last victim in the little upper chamber, pointed forward to the Lamb of God who was to take away the sin of the world. All the washings, and sprinklings, and vestments, and ritual of the law, found their meaning only in Christ, and can be fully interpreted only at the cross.

The prophets spake of him from Enoch to Malachi: Isaiah, sounding his gospel in terms of such unequalled grandeur; Jeremiah, uttering it in tears; Ezekiel, gazing, rapt in astonishment on the Son of Man; Daniel, counting the very weeks until Messiah was to be cut off; Zechariah, proclaiming the lowly king; and Malachi, the refiner and purifier of silver, who should soon come to his temple. "The testimony of Jesus is the spirit of prophecy."

The *psalms*, including all the devotional portions of the Scripture, are also full of rich strains of tenderness and pathos, that find their key note only in the song of Moses and the Lamb.

The burden of all those utterances of revelation was that Christ must suffer and rise from the dead; in other words, must make an atonement by suffering. This is the great cardinal doctrine of the Christian system, a doctrine which every age has seen attacked, and yet to which every age has been compelled at last to return, as the living, throbbing heart of the gospel. As the sense of sin grows faint in an individual or an age, the need of atonement is less deeply felt, and a mere symbolical, or figurative atonement is adopted instead of a real, vicarious substitution. But when the sense of sin grows deeper, and its intrinsic ill-desert is more clearly perceived, then this great doctrine of revelation begins to glow as if with light from heaven, that it behoved Christ both to suffer, and to rise again from the dead; since his suffering was needed as an atonement, and his resurrection as an authentication of this great transaction, from the hand of God himself. It is most marvellous that this most sublime and touching act of love should be charged with the implication that it presents God in an implacable and unamiable light, as unwilling to forgive, when God had emptied his very throne, in a measure, to show that he was willing and waiting to forgive. It shows that sin is a great and horrible evil, and that God is a God of inflexible justice and truth; it shows that mere repentance, without atonement, can never procure pardon; but it also shows that God is merciful and full of love, as nothing else ever did, for he had but one Son, his well-beloved, and that Son he gave to suffer, that sinners might be saved.

Hence we learn the true nature and position of repentance. Repentance can procure pardon only after an atonement is made. And true repentance is only exercised by resting on the atonement. Here we find the test that distinguishes true and false repentance. False repentance is sin weeping because of the suffering that it has brought upon itself. True repentance is love weeping at the cross, its bitterest tears being wrung out by the fact that it has sinned against a goodness that can so freely, and yet at so costly a price, bestow a full and generous pardon. Hence we see why repentance and remission of sins could then be preached, as the result of the suffering and re-surrection of Jesus Christ.

If then an atonement for sin is the great central doctrine of revelation, it is the great central fact of history, for the plan of God's redeeming work is the most memorable part of his

earthly government. Hence human history is one mighty ora-
torio of the Messiah, whose deep bass notes are the solemn
and suffering tones which proclaim man a great sinner, and
whose lofty alto is sounded by those glorious strains which
proclaim Christ a great Saviour, and whose choral song
bursts forth in the grand Hallelujah, "Glory to God in the
highest, and on earth peace and good will to men." In the din
and discord that are around us now, we cannot catch the
mighty harmonies that run through the whole; but when we
come to trace it from the great choral company around the
throne, we shall then know, as we cannot now, how the song
of the morning stars at the dawn of creation, and the song of
the angels on the plains of Bethlehem, and the song of Moses
and the Lamb, the new song in heaven, were all one and the
same great melody, the wondrous harmony of justice and
mercy, sin and salvation, righteousness and peace, by the
work of Him who loved us and gave himself for us, and
redeemed us by his blood.

3. *A Divine power is needful to enable man to comprehend
the gospel of Christ.*

This appears from the statement of Luke, in v. 45. "Then
opened he their understanding, that they might understand
the scriptures." The influence of the Spirit here bestowed was
doubtless an extraordinary one, qualifying them to be unerring interpreters of the Scriptures already written, and writers
of those yet unwritten. But this fact involves a wider truth.
There was no peculiar blindness in their case requiring any
peculiar "opening of the understanding." There is a darken-
ing of the understanding that is common to all, for by nature
man is not only guilty but blind. "The natural man receiveth
not the things of the Spirit of God, for they are foolishness
unto him; neither can he know them, because they are spiritually discerned." 1 Cor. 2.14. Hence in the great work of
regeneration, there is more than a mere increase of light;
there is an opening of the blind eyes to see the light, before

that light can be of any use. Hence David prayed, "Open thou mine eyes, that I may behold wondrous things out of thy law." Ps. 119.18. Isaiah predicted the Messiah as one who was "to open the blind eyes," ch. 42. 7, and in the actual work of the gospel, "The Lord opened the heart of Lydia." Acts 16.14.

It is this blindness that leads men to prefer sin to holiness. If the eyes were open, they would as soon prefer a cancer or a leprosy for the body, as prefer sin for the soul. And it is this blindness that leads men to neglect the gospel with its grandeur and beauty, neglect the Bible with its unparalleled attractions, and neglect God the loveliest, most glorious, and purest, as he is the holiest and greatest of all objects of thought or affection. Hence, however cogently truth may be presented to the understanding, its real beauty and power can never be seen until the Spirit of God opens the blind eyes, and enables them to see. Then as the light dawns, a new world is unveiled, a world all bathed in sunlight from heaven, and all things become new. The Bible is seen to be a new book, and its pages glow with a splendour that was never seen before. The whole past, present, and future of life are seen in another light, and in that new light, the soul begins its pilgrimage to that better country, the road to which begins at the cross, and ends in that city that hath foundations, whose builder and maker is God. To enable us to see this blessed path, our cry must be that of the blind Bartimaeus, "Lord, that I may receive my sight."

4. *The salvation of the gospel is for all, however remote their habitation, or great their sin.*

"Among all nations beginning at Jerusalem," presents the limitations placed by Jesus himself to his gospel. Among these "all nations," then far distant, were our fathers, then in heathenism, if not barbarism; and it is by this universal warrant that the gospel was brought to them, and thus handed down to us. Had the apostles felt about the heathen of their day, as many feel about the heathen of this day, the gospel could never have reached us, and we must have been yet in our sins. It was missionary labour that brought the gospel to us, and it must be by the same kind of work that it is to be carried to others. Hence the enjoyment of the gospel by us carries with it the express condition that we should transmit it to others, even to all nations; and until all nations have received it, cessation of missionary labour is disobedience to Christ.

But if the command to carry the gospel to "all nations" implies that no one is debarred from its blessings by remoteness of habitation, the command to begin at Jerusalem indicates the same free offer, however great the sin. There is something very touching in this injunction to begin at Jerusalem. We would have thought beforehand that if there were any place that must be excluded, it would be Jerusalem. It was over Jerusalem he had uttered those words of doom, "But now they are hid from thine eyes." It was of Jerusalem that he had exclaimed, "Thou that killest the prophets and stonest them who are sent to thee." It was along the streets of Jerusalem that the wild and bloody cry for blood, rang with such fiendish ferocity, "Crucify him, crucify him!" It was the soil of Jerusalem that was wet with the tears and sweat of Gethsemane, and the blood and water of Calvary. Hence if there were any spot on earth that might expect the sternest exclusion from the blessings of the gospel, that spot was Jerusalem. But the wonderful fact is, that it was to this very spot, all stained with guilt, that the first offer was to be made. And why? Because their guilt was not so deeply dyed? Oh, no, but just because its dye was so deep and indelible; for if Jerusalem, all red with the blood of prophets and martyrs, and last of all, the priceless blood of the well-beloved Son—if Jerusalem could be forgiven, none need despair. If Jerusalem can be saved, none need be lost. This is the sublime and tender assurance of this injunction. If a soul feels its sins to be too heavy and dark, it only needs that we point to the fact that the offer

of mercy was to begin at Jerusalem, to show that no sin, however deeply dyed, can exclude from pardon, if the sinner will
come with a penitent heart to Christ.

Bunyan in his quaint tract on these words, entitled, "The
Jerusalem sinner saved, or Good news for the vilest of men,"
gives in his dramatic vein, a lively picture of the fulfilment of
this part of the commission. He represents Peter declaring to
the people of Jerusalem the message, "Repent and be baptized, *every one of you*," and the people urging their objections. "*Obj.* But I was one of them that plotted to take away
his life: may I be saved by him? *Peter*. Every one of you. *Obj.*
But I was one of them that bare false witness against him: is
there grace for me? *Peter*. For every one of you. *Obj.* But I
was one of them that cried out, Crucify, crucify him, and that
desired that Barabbas the murderer might live rather than
him: what will become of me, think you? *Peter*. I am to
preach repentance and remission of sins to every one of you.
Obj. But I was one of them that did spit in his face when he
stood before his accusers; I also was one that mocked him,
when in anguish he hanged bleeding on the tree: is there room
for me? *Peter*. For every one of you. *Obj.* But I was one of
them that in his extremity said, Give him gall and vinegar to
drink: why may I not expect the same, when anguish and
guilt is upon me? *Peter*. Repent of these your wickednesses,
and here is remission of sins for every one of you."

And yet deep as was the guilt of these Jerusalem sinners, the
very atrocity of their guilt when pardon is offered, makes the
guilt of impenitence and rejection of the gospel now to be yet
more atrocious. If it will be more tolerable for Sodom and
Gomorrah in the great day, than for Chorazin, Bethsaida,
and Capernaum, it will be more tolerable for the Jerusalem
sinner than for many in our day. For he may well say to the
soul that rejects Christ now, "I never knew that the crucified
Jesus was the Saviour of sinners, I rejected him ignorantly in
unbelief, not knowing that he was the Holy One of Israel; I

never read the pages of the New Testament, unfolding so richly the great ideas of the Old; I never saw the stupendous mass of evidence that eighteen centuries of history have piled around the cross; I never had a Christian mother to whisper of the babe of Bethlehem in my childhood, or a Christian father to tell me of the man of Calvary in riper years; had I enjoyed all these, I would long since have repented in dust and ashes." And the force of this plea is undeniable. Hence it may be that if the offer of mercy was to begin at Jerusalem, so also must the sentence of doom. It may be that as the long line of unhappy souls begins to file away from the left hand of the Judge, and take their places in the dark chambers of the damned, the same rule may be applied then that was applied at the opening of the gospel, "beginning at Jerusalem," and ending with those who have been nurtured in Christian homes, instructed in Christian churches, and yet who have refused themselves to be Christian disciples. It may be that some of these may be compelled to say to the guilty sons and daughters of Jerusalem, "Give me room to sink to a deeper, darker, hotter doom than even that beginning at Jerusalem; for as much higher as have been my privileges, so much deeper must be my doom."

CHAPTER 18

THE TENTH APPEARANCE—APOSTOLIC COMMISSION IN ACTS

The gospel of the Holy Ghost. I. *Waiting for the promise of the Father.* Gorgeous dreams of the kingdom—Curiosity about the future—Almanac makers of prophecy—Waiting for the vision—Creation groaning—How must we wait? II. *The promise of the Father.* Meaning of baptism—Mode of baptism—The dispensation of the Spirit—Christ's ascent the condition of the Spirit's descent—Intercession of the Holy Ghost, how it differs from that of Christ. III. *Effects of the fulfilment of the promise.* All Christians witnesses for Christ—Passive witnessing—Martyrs—Cecil and his mother, Addison—The unconscious witness.

> "Eternal Spirit, we confess,
> And sing the wonders of thy grace:
> Thy power conveys our blessings down,
> From God the Father, and the Son.
> The troubled conscience knows thy voice,
> Thy cheering words awake our joys,
> Thy words allay the stormy wind,
> And calm the surges of the mind."

"The former treatise have I made, O Theophilus, of all that Jesus began both to do and teach, until the day in which he was taken up, after that he through the Holy Ghost had given commandments unto the apostles whom he had chosen: to whom also he shewed himself alive after his passion by many infallible proofs, being seen of them forty days, and speaking of the things pertaining to the kingdom of God: and being assembled together with them, commanded them that they should not depart from Jerusalem, but wait for the promise of the Father, which saith he, ye have heard of me. For John truly baptized with water; but ye shall be baptized with the Holy Ghost not many days hence. When they therefore were come together, they asked of him, saying, Lord, wilt thou at this time restore again the kingdom to Israel? And he said

unto them, It is not for you to know the times or the seasons, which
the Father hath put in his own power. But ye shall receive power,
after that the Holy Ghost is come upon you: and ye shall be witnesses unto me both in Jerusalem, and in all Judea, and in Samaria,
and unto the uttermost part of the earth." Acts 1.1-8.

We have now reached the last form in which the apostolic
commission was issued by the Holy Spirit, and the last record
that was made of this closing interview between Jesus and his
disciples. We have seen how precisely each of the preceding
forms of the commission was adapted to the purpose of the
Gospel in which it is found. It will, of course, not be supposed
for a moment that it is designed to represent either as an
inaccurate statement of the words of our Lord. It has already
been stated, that the probability is that our Lord spent all the
night preceding the ascension with his disciples, and that he
said very many things that have not been recorded, and said
the same thing in different forms, leaving each writer to
select that portion of his discourse that was most suitable to
the object of his narrative. Hence there being a necessity, in
the existing condition of the world, and in the great representative nations then most prominent, for different utterances
of the same facts, the same necessity required correspond-
ingly different presentations of the apostolic commission.
Matthew, in writing for the Hebrews, gave such portion of
the discourse as was most suitable to the Hebrew mind. Mark,
writing for the Romans, gave the form demanded by their
peculiar condition. Luke, when writing a Gospel, with a view
to the wants of the Greeks, gave one form of the commission;
but in writing the Acts, having a different object in view, he
gives us other facts omitted in the former record. As this book
was written more than thirty years after the facts occurred,
and when the church was in a very different condition from
that in which it was at first, we look with interest at the statement of facts which it was deemed necessary to place on
record in this last narrative of the history. The Acts of the

Apostles has been called the Gospel of the Holy Ghost, from the prominence given to that Divine agent in the book. We find this very feature in the record of the commission. Whilst the portion of our Lord's words quoted by Luke, in his Gospel, mentions the Scriptures three times, we find here the same number of allusions to the Holy Ghost, thus giving us a clue to the great object of this fifth Gospel. The design of the book, and of the form of the commission given in the book, is to present prominently the great fact that the New Testament dispensation is pre-eminently a dispensation of the Holy Ghost. We have also the further facts not mentioned elsewhere, that our Lord tarried on earth forty days after his resurrection, holding many conversations with his disciples, and that the topic of them all was the kingdom of God, which he had come on earth to set up. There are several points here deserving our attention.

1. *Waiting for the promise of the Father.*

Christ "commanded them that they should not depart from Jerusalem, but wait for the promise of the Father, which, saith he, ye have heard of me." Here is one of the most difficult duties to which a Christian is ever summoned. To work for the promise is easy, to wait for it is often very hard. There is a restless eagerness to enjoy what is hoped for, that makes us uneasy under any delay in the fulfilment of the promise.

This feeling we detect in the question of the disciples, "Lord, wilt thou at this time restore again the kingdom to Israel?" It is plain from this question that there was not a little carnality still in their views. Trammelled by their traditional and national expectations, they could not fully comprehend, either the promise of the Father, or the nature of the kingdom of God. They expected evidently a temporal, rather than a spiritual kingdom. Burning with the glorious memories of the past when the magnificence of David and Solomon shed on Israel a splendour that outshone the glory of all the rest of the earth, and secretly chafing under the crushing yoke of Rome, they looked and longed for the great Deliverer, who was to unfurl the banner of David on the hills of Judea; and rallying, with the war-cry of the past, all the true sons of Israel would sweep from her hallowed soil every trace of the haughty invader, and again make Jerusalem a joy of the whole earth. Impatient for these glorious destinies, they were eager to rush to the conflict. Hence they asked whether at this time he meant to restore the old kingly line, and with it the kingly splendour, to Israel.

As the question was only in regard to the time, and not in regard to the nature of the kingdom, and as the lesson to be taught was the lesson of patiently waiting for the promise, whether it was clearly understood or not, our Lord confines his reply to the single point raised in the question, "It is not for you to know the times or the seasons which the Father hath put in his own power." He knew that the teachings of the Holy Ghost would soon explain to them the nature of the kingdom. His single aim was to reprove that impatient desire that they manifested to wrest from the future its untold secrets, and read the chronology of that book that God alone can open and peruse.

The feeling here reproved is by no means an unusual one, nor is it yet extinct. There has been always, and is now in many minds, an intense desire to lift the veil that hides the future, and force on the wheels of the ark of God. It sometimes appears in a very offensive form, selecting certain delusive data of prophetic interpretation, and then predicting the very day and hour when the Son of Man shall come; startling for a while the credulous and superstitious, but in the end hardening men more obdurately in scepticism and sin. The gross delusion of Millerism[1] in our times is an illustration, and some very popular expositors of prophecy incur some-

---

[1] The 19th-century adventist movement, named after its founder who believed the return of Christ would take place in 1843.

what of the same condemnation that rests on these grosser forms of enthusiasm and error.

There is a time when the great purposes of God shall be finished, and, especially, when the last awful appearance shall be made. But this time is wisely concealed by God, in order that no man or generation may be lulled into presumption. It is designed that the end of the world to the race, may be like the end of the world to the individual: certain in its event, that all may prepare for it; uncertain in its time, that this preparation may not be postponed, and life lost and wasted in sin. Hence to those who would wring from prophetic data the precise year and day of the coming of Christ, and most of those data the very revelations that the disciples had when they asked Christ this question, *i. e.*, the prophecies of Daniel, we may very properly reply, "It is not for you to know the times and seasons which the Father hath put in his own power." Of that day and hour knoweth no man, not even the Son in his human and prophetic capacity, for it is not designed to be revealed to any mere creature in his simple capacity as a creature. Hence this prurient desire to wring from the sublime symbolism of prophecy the exact dates of a table of chronology, is at once a folly and a crime.

There is an anxiety as to what is coming, that is lawful and commendable. This feeling expresses itself in the prayers, "Thy kingdom come." "Come, Lord Jesus, come quickly," "How long, O Lord, holy and true, dost thou not judge and avenge our blood on them that dwell on the earth?" This anxiety will lead us to labour and to hope. But when this anxiety rises into impatience; when the slow progress of the gospel makes us grow weary in the work of spreading it; when the little fruit that we see tempts us to cease our efforts to plant and to water the seed; when we are ready to say it is useless to work on when that work seems to be so utterly in vain; then we reach a point of anxiety that is sinful, and have some of the feeling reproved in the disciples. We would have the promise fulfilled *"at this time,"* now, and unwilling to wait in patience, and need then to be reminded that it is not for us to know the times and seasons that the Father has put in his own power. To work and to wait are ours, to promise and to perform are God's; and as surely as we do the first, so surely will he, at the best possible time, do the last.

There is a promise of the Father for which the whole earth groaneth and travaileth together in pain, until now. This glorious "manifestation of the sons of God" will be the end of all toils and pains to the struggling and divided church of God. It is not to be wondered at that the weary heart will sometimes cry out in impatience, "How long, O Lord, how long?" It is then that this calm and commanding word "wait" comes clear and comforting to our souls. "The vision is yet for an appointed time, but at the end it shall speak and not lie: though it tarry, wait for it, because it will surely come, it will not tarry." The sublime outgoings of the eternal kingdom are governed by their own immutable laws, and these laws are beyond our finite and feeble ken. "One day is with the Lord as a thousand years, and a thouand years as one day. The Lord is not slack concerning his promise as some men count slackness, but is long-suffering." 2 Pet. 3.8, 9.

But how must we wait? In idleness? In slumber? No; we must wait as the husbandman waits for the early and latter rains, who labours while he waits; wait as the watchman waits for the dawn, who watches as he waits; wait as the wise virgins waited, who trimmed their lamps as they waited, and kept oil in their vessels with their lamps. We know how the disciples waited, and thus also are we to wait. They waited in prayer, not merely secret but social and united prayer, and so must we. They waited in labour, striving to do all that they could to be ready for the blessing, and so must we. They waited in love and united action, being all with one accord in one place, and so must we. They waited in holy seclusion from the world, wrestling with God for the promise, and so must we. They waited in faith, assuredly looking for the gift of the Holy Ghost, and so must we. Pentecostal prayer must always precede a pentecostal blessing.

These general principles are applicable to every promise of the Father, and every object of hope for which we are to wait in hope. Do we long for the conversion of our children? We must wait, but work and watch and pray while we wait. Is it for some personal blessing, some attainment in the divine life? We must wait, but wrestle while we wait, strive to subdue the besetting sin, and to draw down from God the promised blessing. Is it in some department of labour that we wait? The pastor, the elder, the teacher, the parent have often to wait long before they see the result of their labours. But they should wait as Israel waited for the fall of the walls of Jericho, in simple obedience to the commands of God. Is it for a larger outpouring of the Spirit? We must wait as Elijah waited on Carmel, praying while we wait, and looking while we pray, and fainting not though the cloud be but as a man's hand, and afar off on the distant sea. Is it for the first great blessing in religion, a new heart, and a hope in Christ? Many wait for this in a very sinful way. They wait, hoping that God will do what they must do, and give them the conscious possession of a new heart before they submit themselves to Christ and cast themselves on his mercy. But they must wait in believing, wait in repenting, wait in praying, and wait in obeying, and they will not wait in vain. Man cannot make the seed sprout, but he may sow it, and he must sow it before he can expect it to grow. God must give the increase, but man must plant and water, or there will be no increase. Hence in every duty, difficulty, danger, perplexity, and sorrow, the rule is the same; we must wait, but wait in faith, hope, obedience, and labour, and we shall not wait in vain.

2. *The promise of the Father*.

The promise is fully explained. "For John truly baptized

with water, but ye shall be baptized with the Holy Ghost not many days hence." v. 5. "But ye shall receive power after that the Holy Ghost is come upon you." v. 8. The promise of the Father is therefore the gift of the Holy Ghost. It was promised to Christ as a reward for his mediatorial sufferings, and that which the Father gave to the Son, the Son gave to the church and world, when he ascended on high, leading captivity captive, and obtaining gifts for men. In the form of the promise here given, there are several points of deep interest involved.

We learn something of the meaning of the ordinance of baptism. The contrast that Christ draws between baptism with water, and baptism with the Holy Ghost, shows that he regards the one as symbolical of the other, and the water baptism to be the sign and seal of the work of the Holy Ghost. The Holy Spirit is here presented to us under three great emblems in Scripture, air, fire, and water: air, implying life; fire, purity; and water, combining both in a certain sense, being equally necessary for life and purity of body.

As water both slakes the burning thirst of man and revives the parching fields, and also purifies whilst it cools and refreshes, so is the agency of the Spirit on the soul. Hence this outward application of water is designed to symbolize the inward application of the life-giving and purifying influences of the Holy Ghost. As the Lord's supper then symbolizes the work of the Son, baptism represents the work of the Holy Spirit, thus giving a complete exhibition of the great work of redemption and regeneration, by which we are made meet for the inheritance of the saints in light.

We also learn something as to the proper mode of baptism. Without entering at large on this vexed question, we cannot avoid noticing the decisive facts of this passage. The influences of the Holy Spirit are very often represented as being "poured" on the recipient. The anointings of the Old Testament, which represented the influences of the Spirit, were made always by pouring oil on the head. (See Ps. 133.2; Luke 4.18, &c.) These influences are so represented always in the Old Testament, as in Isa. 32.15, "Until the Spirit be poured upon us from on high." In the New Testament the same representation is uniformly given. The Spirit is said to "come" on the recipient, Acts 1.8; 2.2; to be "poured," Acts 2.16-18; 10.45; to be "shed," Acts 2.33; to "fall on," Acts 10.44; 11.15; and similar expressions, of the same import. Hence whatever might have been the usage of the world before this time, it is plain that they must have inferred that if baptism by the Holy Ghost was to take place by the pouring of the Holy Ghost upon the subject, baptism by water (which was to be exactly like it by the express words of Jesus) must be done by the pouring of water on the subject. When the resemblance between the two baptisms was presented so strongly, if the one must be by pouring, surely so must be the other. Now as they were familiar with a use of water called a baptism, done in the same way, the baptism of tables, couches, &c., (Mark 7.4, 8; Luke 11.38,) the natural inference is that the baptism by water was done "as" the baptism of the Holy Ghost, that is, by pouring on the subject. Hence this we believe to have been the primitive mode of baptism, though laid aside when superstition began to creep into the church, and attach some saving efficacy to mere outward rites, and especially to the sacraments, at which time the washing of the whole body took the place of the simpler mode of the early church.

But the great fact presented in the promise was that the New Testament dispensation was to be one of the Spirit. There are depths of truth here which we can but imperfectly grasp, and on which we should meditate with profound reverence. But our Lord states a fact so emphatically and repeatedly that we cannot mistake its meaning. He says that he must depart from the earth before the Spirit could descend in power. This is reiterated in the Gospel of John. (See ch. 14.16, 17, 26; 15.26; 16.7, 13.) If he did not return to heaven, the

Spirit would not come down to earth. The reason for this necessity we cannot fully understand. It may be that the whole plan of redemption is designed to set forth the sublime mystery of the Trinity, that as the one God, the Father, was most prominent before the incarnation, the Son revealed in the incarnation and life of Jesus on earth, so the Spirit was to be revealed in the next great phase, the life of the church on earth; and thus that human history in its relation to the work of redemption was designed to shadow forth the deep mysteries of the Godhead, and show that all spiritual blessings must be *from* the Father, *through* the Son, and *by* the Holy Ghost.

Whatever be the remote reason of the fact, the fact itself stands clearly out, that the New Testament dispensation is pre-eminently the dispensation of the Spirit. And the words of Jesus intimate that it was needful that he should make the grand triumphal entrance of the ascension, and be inaugurated as the King of glory above, before the Spirit could be poured out below; and that this great descent of the Holy One was to be the signal on earth that the mighty transaction in heaven had taken place, the everlasting doors been lifted up, and the King of glory entered in to his mediatorial throne in heaven. Hence, now we are to look for all blessings through the Son as their medium, but by the Holy Spirit as their applying agency. The Scriptures, to which we come for words of eternal life, are inspired by the Holy Ghost. Regeneration, the beginning of the spiritual life, is the work of the Holy Ghost. Sanctification, the progress of the spiritual life, is by the agency of the Holy Ghost. Prayer, the breath of the spiritual life, is by the aid, often in "groanings that cannot be uttered," of the Holy Ghost. Good works, the proof and product of the spiritual life, are the fruits of the Holy Ghost. The whole work of the spiritual life is the work of the Holy Ghost. As Christ is a Mediator with the Father to bring us to him, the Holy Ghost is a mediator between the soul and Christ to draw us to Jesus, and enable us to lay hold of him by faith.

Here we reach a most important fact that is often over-looked, the intercession of the Holy Ghost. We think almost exclusively of the intercession of Christ, forgetting that there is another intercession that is also most priceless to us, and should ever be cherished. There is an important distinction between these two intercessions, though a distinction but lit-tle regarded. Christ intercedes as Mediator with God; the Holy Spirit, as Paraclete, Pleader, with man. Christ inter-cedes as a Priest, completing the sacrificial and sacerdotal work which he assumed as our representative; the Holy Spirit, as an applier of this priestly work to the human heart. Christ intercedes with the Father on the ground of his merit, having purchased a right to the travail of his soul; the Holy Spirit, on the ground of compassion, pleading only the guilt and ruin of man. Christ intercedes in heaven; the Holy Spirit, on earth.

Hence we are brought to a most touching fact in our spiri-tual relations, that a double intercession is ever going on in regard to us, if we are God's children; Christ making interces-sion by his blood in heaven, the Holy Spirit making interces-sion for us, with groanings that cannot be uttered, on earth; the one at the throne of glory above, the other at the throne of grace below; the one preparing a place for us in the inheri-tance of the saints in light, the other preparing us for that place, by working in us a meetness for this heavenly inheri-tance. The promise of the Father, therefore, for which the dis-ciples were to wait, was the great blessing of the New Testa-ment, the great hope of a sinful world, the great reliance of a struggling church, the influences of the Holy Spirit, by which, "convincing us of our sin and misery, enlightening our minds in the knowledge of Christ, and renewing our wills, he doth persuade and enable us to embrace Jesus Christ, freely offered to us in the gospel," and by which "we are renewed in the whole man after the image of God, and enabled more and more to die unto sin, and live unto righteousness."

3. *Effects of the fulfilment of the promise.*

"Ye shall be witnesses unto me, both in Jerusalem, and in Judea, and in Samaria, and unto the uttermost part of the earth."

There is a peculiar sense in which the apostles were to be witnesses for Christ, as they were to attest his resurrection from the dead from their own personal knowledge. Hence they must have seen the risen Saviour. And in their writings, they are witnesses to the ends of the earth.

But there is a sense in which all Christians are included in this testifying character, for all are witnesses for Christ, and thus only can this witness be carried to the uttermost part of the earth.

Each Christian, by his life, must be a witness for Christ, and show that he has been with Jesus, and learned of him. Some are to witness for him in the pulpit, some in the pews, some in the city, some in the wilderness, some at home, some far hence away among the heathen, some in the parlour, some in the kitchen, some in the nursery, some in the senate; but all required to bear the same testimony, that "Christ is the power of God, and the wisdom of God unto salvation, to all them that believe." To bear false witness against our neighbour is a great sin, but to bear false witness for Christ, is much more fearful, for the man who does this lies, not against man, but against God.

But there is a passive witnessing for Christ as well as an active, and often a much harder testimony to bear. So important is this kind of witnessing, that the word martyr, which means witness, has been appropriated in common language to this kind of witnessing for Christ. Richard Cecil relates that it was the example of his mother in enduring affliction with so much patience, that convinced him of the reality of religion, when he was a sceptical and godless youth. Lying one night in bed he reflected thus, as he records in his life: "I see two unquestionable facts. First, my mother is greatly afflicted in circumstances, body and mind, and yet I see that she cheerfully bears up under all, by the support she derives from constantly retiring to her closet and Bible. Secondly, that she has a secret spring of comfort of which I know nothing, while I, who give an unbounded loose to my appetites, and seek pleasure by every means, seldom or never find it. If however there is any such secret in religion, why may not I attain it as well as my mother? I will immediately seek it of God." He did seek it, and found it in Jesus.

Thus it often is in cases that will never be known fully until "the books" are opened. The humble, poor, and suffering Christian, who bears in loneliness and poverty the sufferings of life, is testifying to all around the power of Christ, as really, and often as successfully, as Paul in the midst of Mars' Hill. If it was an impressive witness for the power of religion that was given by the great English essayist, when he sent for his nephew to see in what peace a Christian can die, it is a more impressive testimony that is given by some poor lonely, neglected sufferer, who, without feeling that she is acting a part for the inspection of the world, yet in obscurity and desertion, shows to those who are permitted to watch her daily life, with what patience a Christian can suffer. She may testify for Christ in her poverty and sickness, with more powerful effect than the most eloquent orator in the pulpit, for she *is* what he only describes. Hence in every department of life, in joy and sorrow, we are able to be witnesses for Christ, and testify by our conduct what the Lord has done for our souls; and as the circle of Christian influence widens, this witness shall at last be carried to the uttermost part of the earth.

CHAPTER 19

THE ASCENSION

Why the Ascension is so little alluded to in Scripture. I. *The fact of the Ascension.* (1) The time. (2) The place. (3) The attendant circumstances. II. *The reasons for the Ascension.* (1) The Priesthood of Christ. (2) The entrance into glory after suffering. (3) To display his Divine nature. (4) Connection with the descent of the Holy Ghost. (5) His intercession. (6) Preparing a place for us. (7) Our forerunner and example—His ascension the picture and pledge of ours. (8) Sitting at the right hand of God—The Pilgrim.

> "Soft cloud, that while the breeze of May
> Chants her glad matins in the leafy arch,
> Draw'st thy bright veil across the heavenly way,
> Meet pavement for an angel's glorious march;
> My soul is envious of mine eye,
> That it should soar and glide with thee so fast,
> The while my grovelling thoughts half-buried lie,
> Or lawless roam around this earthly waste.
> Chains of my heart, avaunt, I say—
> I will arise, and in the strength of love,
> Pursue the bright track ere it fade away,
> My Saviour's pathway to his home above."

"So then, after the Lord had spoken unto them, he was received up into heaven, and sat on the right hand of God,"—Mark 16.19.

"And he led them out as far as to Bethany; and he lifted up his hands, and blessed them. And it came to pass, while he blessed them, he was parted from them, and carried up into heaven. And they worshipped him, and returned to Jerusalem with great joy." Luke 24.50-52.

"And when he had spoken these things, while they beheld, he was taken up; and a cloud received him out of their sight. And while they looked steadfastly toward heaven, as he went up, behold, two men stood by them in white apparel; which also said, Ye men of Galilee, why stand ye gazing up into heaven? This same Jesus which is taken up from you into heaven, shall so come in like

manner as ye have seen him go into heaven. Then returned they
unto Jerusalem from the mount called Olivet, which is from Jerusalem a sabbath-day's journey."—Acts 1.9-12.

It is a little remarkable, that an event which strikes us so
forcibly as the Ascension, should not have occupied a larger
space in the sacred records. To us the Ascension is even a
more wonderful event than the Resurrection, and we naturally crave a full account of it, to satisfy our curiosity. But the
sacred writers never attempt to satisfy mere curiosity, or the
demands of imagination. Their silence and reserve are often
more wonderful, and more indicative of divine guidance,
than their revelations. The Ascension is regarded by them as
so closely linked with the Resurrection, so necessarily following it, and so blended with it in significance, that they dwell
much more on the latter than on the former. Hence, whilst all
the gospels record the Resurrection, but two of them record
the Ascension. Mark (16.19) gives a very brief record of it:
"So then, after the Lord had spoken unto them, he was
received up into heaven, and sat on the right hand of God."
Luke, writing at probably a later date, when the importance
of the event was more fully apprehended, gives us a fuller
account of it. In his Gospel (24.50-52) he states: "And he led
them out as far as to Bethany, and he lifted up his hands and
blessed them. And it came to pass, while he blessed them, he
was parted from them, and carried up into heaven. And they
worshipped him, and returned to Jerusalem with great joy."
In the Acts, he gives another account of it—(1.9-12): "And
when he had spoken these things, while they beheld, he was
taken up, and a cloud received him out of their sight. And
while they looked steadfastly toward heaven, as he went up,
behold two men stood by them in white apparel, which also
said, Ye men of Galilee, why stand ye gazing up into heaven?
This same Jesus which is taken up from you into heaven, shall
so come in like manner as ye have seen him go into heaven.

Then returned they unto Jerusalem, from the mount called Olivet, which is from Jerusalem a Sabbath-day's journey." It is alluded to by Paul in several of his larger Epistles: (Eph. 4.8-10; Heb. 10.12;) by Peter twice in his first Epistle; (1 Pet. 1.21; 3.22;) and is implied in the visions of the Apocalypse. Rev. 2.8, &c.

Hence, it is not from any want of evidence as to the fact that it is not more frequently alluded to; but because it is so closely connected with the Resurrection as to stand or fall with it; and because the great contest was necessarily in regard to the first, and not the second event. Admit the Resurrection, and the Ascension will follow without any difficulty.

But, notwithstanding this infrequency of allusion, the Ascension is a most important fact in the life of our Lord, and one that deserves our most careful study. It will be well worth our while to obtain a clear notion of that fact itself, with the reasons for its occurrence, and the results that flow from it.

1. *The fact of the Ascension.*

In looking at the fact, there are three points that claim our attention, and require a brief discussion. They are the time of its occurrence in the life of our Lord, the place of its occurrence, and the attendant circumstances.

(1) The time of its occurrence was forty days after the Resurrection. Why this precise number of days was selected is a matter of mere conjecture. It was forty days after his birth that he was brought to the temple to be dedicated to the Lord by his parents; and during forty days he was tempted in the wilderness, before entering on his public ministry; and during forty days he was to remain on earth after Resurrection, before entering into glory. It may be that these successive periods of forty days were designed to point backward to the forty years' sojourn in the wilderness before entering Canaan; and not only to link these histories together, but also present the same great lesson of a season of painful preparation before entering upon the fulfilment of the promise. There is a

minute interlacing of analogies between the history of the Jewish people, the history of Jesus, and the history of the followers of Jesus, that cannot be wholly undesigned. They seem designed to show the oneness of God's plan of redemption, however various be its outward form of dispensation or administration.

(2) The place of this transaction is stated to have been the Mount of Olives, near Bethany. The Mount of Olives lies between Jerusalem and Bethany. On the one side is the Holy City, separated from it by the valley of Jehoshaphat; on the other is the village of Mary and Martha, separated from the mountain by a little ridge of hills. It was here probably, in the recess furnished by these hills that project from the Mount of Olives and overhang Bethany, that this glorious event occurred. There is a spot on the summit of the mountain, directly in view of the city, which is traditionally designated as the place, and marked by the Chapel of the Ascension. But it is too far from Bethany to meet the terms of the narrative, and too directly in view of the city to comport with the retired character of the event. Hence, the spot that answers best to the narrative is one that is immediately above Bethany, and yet on a projected spur of Olivet. Dean Stanley, in his *Sinai and Palestine*, says of this spot:

"On the wild uplands which immediately overhang the village, he withdrew from the eyes of his disciples, in a seclusion which, perhaps, could nowhere else be found so near the stir of a mighty city—the long ridge of Olivet screening those hills, and those hills the village beneath them, from all sound or sight of the city behind, the view opening only on the wide waste of desert rocks and ever-descending valleys, into the depths of the distant Jordan and its mysterious lake. At this point the last interview took place. 'He led them out as far as Bethany,' and 'they returned,' probably by the direct road, over the summit of Mount Olivet. The appropriateness of the real scene presents a singular contrast to the inappropriateness of that fixed by a later fancy, 'seeking for a sign' on the broad top of the mountain, out of sight of Bethany and in full sight of Jerusalem, and thus in equal contradiction to the letter and the spirit of the gospel narrative."

(3) The facts of the scene are few and simple. He may have been with the disciples in one of those nightly meetings, in an upper chamber, which had before been seasons of so much joy to their hearts; and having given them his lessons of wisdom and love, perhaps until the morning began to break on the hills, he led them forth for the last time over Olivet, until they came to that quiet and secluded spot above the village of Bethany, where he had probably spent many an hour in prayer. There, as the rich glow of the coming day was gilding the mountains, and the earth was waking in the gladness of the morning, he held his parting interview with them, and uttered his last words of benediction. Whilst these words were yet on his lips, and the blessing unfinished, he began slowly and majestically to ascend from the ground, still uttering the accents of benediction; and as he went up, a bright cloud— the Shekinah, the symbol of present Deity, that for so many years hung between the cherubim and above the ark— descended from heaven to meet him, and enfolding him in its encircling brightness, carried him up until he was lost in the far-off blue of the empyrean and disappeared from their sight. As they gazed wistfully upwards, two bright forms appeared suddenly to them, and gently chiding them for this longing, tearful, and perhaps doubtful gaze, assured them that this same Jesus should return from heaven in the same way in which he had gone up thither. Cheered by this assurance, they returned to Jerusalem rejoicing.

2. *The reasons for the Ascension.*

Such being the recorded facts of the Ascension, the question now meets us, Why was this scene in our Lord's history necessary? That it was necessary is proved, not only by the fact that it actually took place, but also by the predictions of it made by our Lord himself, and also by the Old Testament prophets. In the memorable discourse on the way to Emmaus, he said: "O fools, and slow of heart to believe all that the prophets have spoken! Ought not Christ to have suffered these things and to enter into his glory?" The sublime ascription of the 68th Psalm, "Thou hast ascended on high; thou hast led captivity captive; thou hast received gifts for men; yea, for the rebellious also, that the Lord God might dwell among them," is expressly referred to the Ascension by Paul, in Eph. 4.9, 10. After quoting this verse from the Psalm, he says: "Now that he ascended, what is it but that he also descended first into the lower parts of the earth? He that descended is the same also that ascended up far above all heavens, that he might fill all things." Here Paul not only makes the Ascension matter of ancient prophecy, but states that it was necessary in order that Christ "might fill all things." The Epistle to the Hebrews presents similar views, in yet more elaborate detail. Heb. 4.14; 6.20; 9.12, 24; 10.12. When our Lord met Mary Magdalene he refused to allow her to touch him, with the view she then had of his return to life, because he was not yet ascended to his Father. He told her to go to the disciples and tell them, "I ascend unto my Father and your Father, and to my God and your God." And before his death, in the touching farewell discourses recorded in the closing chapters of John, he says: "If ye loved me, ye would rejoice because I said, I go unto the Father; for my Father is greater than I." John 14.28. These passages of Scripture are sufficient to prove that there was an absolute necessity for the Ascension, as a part of that wondrous scheme of redemption which Christ came to fulfil on earth. Wherein then consisted this necessity?

(1) The main grounds of this necessity are found in *the priesthood of Christ*, in the fact that he appeared on earth to make atonement for sin, and that this great work would have been incomplete without the Ascension.

In the Mosiac ritual, which Paul assures us was a "pattern of heavenly things," we have this fact set forth very significantly. The high-priest was required, on the great day of atonement, to enter the holy of holies, and present an offering for sin in the very presence of the Shekinah, sprinkling the mercy-seat with the sacrificial blood, for himself, and then for the people; and as he came forth from that awful presence alive, he gave assurance that the atonement was complete, the offering accepted, and man allowed to have entrance to the presence of God in favour. This was further presented by the Cherubim, which symbolized redeemed man, and dwelt perpetually in the presence of the fiery symbol of Jehovah. This yearly entrance of the high-priest to the most holy place prefigured the entrance of Christ into heaven at his Ascension. For this we have the express assurance of the Epistle to the Hebrews. In the eighth and ninth chapters this point is argued in elaborate detail. After showing (chap. 9.1-6) the peculiar facts of the tabernacle and the entrance of the priests daily into the holy place, he adds, in regard to the most holy place, that into it "went the high priest once every year, not without blood, which he offered for himself and for the errors of the people: the Holy Ghost this signifying that the way into the holiest of all was not yet made manifest. . . . But Christ being come an high-priest of good things to come, by a greater and more perfect tabernacle, . . . he entered in once into the holy place, having obtained eternal redemption for us. For Christ is not entered into the holy places made with hands, which are the figures of the true, but into heaven itself, now to appear in the presence of God for us." Heb. 9.7, 8, 11, 12, 24.

The reason for the fact here asserted is by no means an abstruse one. Man had sinned, and therefore been banished from the presence and favour of God. Heaven was closed to him, and he lost all right to its enjoyments. The law, with its inflexible demands, excluded him, and no work of his own could meet those demands. If he suffered the penalty of that law, there was no space left for hope, since that penalty was the extinction of hope itself—*death, eternal death.* To save man from this penalty; to satisfy the claims of that law, and thus remove the obstacle to an admission to the favour and presence of God in heaven, Jesus assumed this nature that had sinned, and united it in mysterious oneness with his divine nature, that a mediatorial person might be formed capable of this great work, and then obeyed both the precept and the penalty of the law; so that our nature suffered, obeyed, died, rose again, and entered into heaven as a permanent dwelling-place, in the person of this second Adam. Now, every step of this process was demanded before the work was complete in itself, or could be so manifested to us. Had Christ not assumed a human nature, he could not have atoned for the sins of a race with such a nature. Had he not obeyed the precept of the law, it could not have been written that "by the obedience of one man many are made righteous." Had he not died, he could not have redeemed us from the curse of that law, whose penalty was death. Had he not risen from the dead, there would have been no assurance to the world that he did not die for his own sins, and no authoritative declaration from God that his atoning work was accepted, and the penalty of death remitted to those who believe. Hence, his resurrection was needful as God's endorsement of his work, and an assurance from the eternal throne that the law was satisfied.

But suppose this had been all, and Christ had remained on earth, or at least not visibly ascended into heaven, would not the work and the proclamation of it be incomplete? The resurrection only assures us that the penalty of death and banishment from heaven is remitted; but this is not enough. We want to know that our nature is to be admitted to an eternal dwelling-place in heaven, and that it is to be allowed to live for ever in the presence of God above. It was this that we lost by the first Adam, and it is this that we would gain by the second. A mere deliverance from death and hell gives no assurance that we are certainly by this atoning Saviour to be admitted hereafter to heaven. Hence we need another stage in this magnificent work. We need that this great representative nature—God manifest in the flesh, man manifested and represented in the Mediator—that this nature shall visibly and openly ascend into heaven, and remain there, the first-fruits of our perpetual and rightful dwelling in heaven, as in its resurrection it was the first-fruits of them that slept. Thus only is that exiled, doomed, and wandering nature restored to what it lost. It was banished from heaven, and its work of restoration cannot be proclaimed as complete until it has publicly been restored to that dwelling-place in the Person of its great representative. As the first Adam was banished from the paradise below, the second must openly be admitted to the paradise above and *dwell there*, before the dread work of sin is undone, and the world assured that the Son of man has destroyed the works of the devil.

Hence it is most obvious that the Ascension was absolutely necessary. The Resurrection proved, indeed, that the curse of the law was gone, and our nature escaped from hell. But it might still be true that no provision was made to secure our entrance to heaven, and our right to do so might still hang in uncertainty. It was, then, further needful that this representative nature should ascend to heaven, be welcomed to its glittering mansions, and occupy them as a permanent habitation. This was done by the Ascension, and hence, as a completion of the work of redemption, and also as a declaration to the world that it was complete, it was needful that he should thus be received into glory.

The necessity is obvious, then, when we take only this earthward view of it. But there are other views opened up by the Scriptures that we cannot pass by, if we would thoroughly comprehend this transaction.

(2) *His mediatorial office required it.*

There was a glory to be assumed by our Lord after his work of suffering, that demanded this public entrance upon it. In his intercessory prayer, he alludes distinctly and very touchingly to this: "I have glorified thee on the earth: I have finished the work which thou gavest me to do. And now, O Father, glorify thou me with thine own self, with the glory which I had with thee before the world was." John 17. 4, 5. Here he distinctly intimates that there is a glory on which he is now to enter that is a result of his work of redemption. This thought is often alluded to in the New Testament, and especially in the Epistles of Paul. The memorable passage in Philippians (2.5-11) is an elaborate statement of this fact. Heb. 1.1-4 states the same truth, and Eph. 4.7-10 is but another presentation of the same thing. There are facts in heaven thus intimated that we can but imperfectly comprehend. There are faint and far-off glimpses of a mighty coronation-day in the heavenly kingdom, of a glittering triumphal entrance into the city that hath foundations; when from the long and far-flashing ranks of the heavenly hosts there went up the shout, "Lift up your heads, O ye gates, and be ye lifted up, ye everlasting doors, and the King of glory shall come in;" and when to the lofty challenge of the one choir of rejoicing ones, "Who is this King of glory?" there came the responsive strain, like the voice of many waters, "The Lord, strong and mighty, the Lord mighty in battle;" and when the ascending Redeemer entered into his glory, sat down on the right hand of God, and assumed the sceptre of his mediatorial kingdom, and entered on that royal authority which he shall hold to the end: "For he must reign till he hath put all enemies under his feet." Hence the Ascension was necessary, that there should be a display in heaven of his mediatorial glory in the assumption of that kingly rule that he is now exercising, and will continue to exercise until the work of redemption is done.

(3) But it is equally required *to display his Divine majesty as the God-man, the Eternal Son.* Had he remained on earth,

it is possible that the world might have grasped the great doctrines of his Divinity, and of the Trinity of Persons in the Godhead, that are now so clear. But it is most probable that it
would have been with difficulty. Were he to appear in all his
Divine glory, as he does in heaven, the whole character of the
dispensation as one of faith would have been changed, and
heaven robbed of one of its strongest attractions. Were he to
appear in the ordinary form of humanity, it would be a perpetual humiliation, implying that his work of atonement was
yet incomplete; and it would have been most difficult for men
to believe that this lowly man, doomed to an undying humiliation on earth, was in very deed the Son of God. But when he
has been visibly taken to heaven, and welcomed by rejoicing
angels; when the pillar of fire, after many centuries' absence
from Jerusalem, descends to carry him in its chariot of glory
to the upper skies; and when he is unveiled to us at the martyrdom of Stephen, and in the visions of the Apocalypse, as at
the right hand of God and in the midst of the throne, we have
no difficulty in believing that he is indeed "God over all,
blessed for ever." Hence, just so far as a revelation of the
Divinity of the Son is needful to man, was the Ascension, by
which that evidence was made complete, a necessary event.

(4) Another necessity for it is found *in its connection with
the work of the Holy Spirit.* What the reason of this connection is, we are probably unable to comprehend, but the fact is
very clear that the Ascension of Christ was a necessary preliminary to the descent of the Holy Ghost. This he asserts
himself in the most explicit terms: "It is expedient for you that
I go away; for if I go not away, the Comforter will not come
unto you; but if I depart, I will send him unto you." John
16.7. So also in John 7.39, it is stated, "The Holy Ghost was
not yet given, because that Jesus was not yet glorified." Why
this is true we cannot tell with any degree of certainty, for we
see but dimly the wondrous arrangements of the Divine economy. It may be that the Spirit could not work, in his pleni-

tude, until the redemption was completed, and the Son acknowledged in heaven as the Lamb slain from the foundation of the world. But the fact is clear, that the Ascension must take place before the Spirit could descend in his New Testament power. Then just as priceless to the world as is the work of the Blessed Paraclete, inspiring the tongues and pens of holy apostles and evangelists; regenerating and converting the thousands that were dead in trespasses and in sins; comforting and sanctifying the suffering people of God; and dwelling in the hearts of the saints, and making their very bodies to be temples more hallowed than that of Moriah—just as absolutely necessary to the Church and to the world as are the gifts and graces of the Holy Comforter, so necessary was that Ascension of Jesus, without which he could not descend in pentecostal or in New Testament power. Hence, the very offices of the Church to which men are called by the Holy Spirit, are placed by the apostle, in Eph. 4.8-12, as among the Ascension gifts of our Lord, when he led captivity captive and obtained gifts for men.

(5) Another reason that the Scriptures give for the Ascension is, that Christ might make *intercession* for us. Paul assures us in Heb. 9.24, "that Christ is entered into heaven itself, now to appear in the presence of God for us;" and (7.25) that he "ever liveth to make intercession for us;" and Rom. 8.34, that he is at the right hand of God, making intercession for us. He is also said to be "an Advocate with the Father." What is the precise nature of that mysterious transaction which is here alluded to, we in our blindness cannot tell. But it is a sweet thought to the trembling sinner, who fears, like the publican, to come even near to the altar, that there is One beside the throne who is interceding for him with that "blood of sprinkling that speaketh better things than the blood of Abel;" and that "if any man sin, we have an Advocate with the Father, even Jesus Christ the righteous. We come then, in our feebleness and frailty, to a throne of grace,

with a more cheering encouragement, when we know that we come not alone, but that a heavenly Pleader is interceding for us, presenting our prayers and struggles before the throne covered with his own infinite merits, and that him the Father always heareth. To enable him to thus intercede, it was needful that he should ascend.

(6) Another reason that he gives himself is, that there was a work of *preparation* for his people to be done in heaven. "In my Father's house are many mansions: if it were not so, I would have told you. I go *to prepare a place* for you." John 14.2. Here again we are at fault as we attempt to grasp these high themes. What is meant by preparing a place for us? Is not heaven already garnished with a glory that was from the foundation of the world? Is it not the perfection of beauty? How, then, could it be prepared for us more gloriously than it always has been? The answer to these queries is probably found in the fact that our place in heaven will be determined by our lives on earth. He whose pound has gained ten pounds shall have rule over ten cities; he that has gained five, but five; he that has gained two, but over two cities. As is the cross, so shall be the crown. As is the burden and heat of the day on earth, so is the exceeding great and eternal weight of glory in heaven. Oh! it is a blessed thought to the toiling and faithful servant of Jesus, that though homeless and penniless below, without a place to lay his head, as he labours for his Master, that precisely as his place on earth is lonely and weary by reason of his faithful working for Christ, by the same, yea, an infinitely greater ratio, is that blessed Saviour preparing a place of peopled loveliness and eternal glory for him above. Then we can see why he told his sorrowing disciples, who shrank from the toil and trial before them, that it became them rather to rejoice that he was about to leave them and ascend to his Father's house, with its many mansions; for there, as they were toiling in weariness and tears, he was preparing for them a warmer, brighter welcome, that

they might be glad according to the years in which they had been made to see sorrow. For this work of preparation, it was needful that he should ascend.

(7) Another reason given by Paul is, that as our *forerunner* and great example, it was needful that he should enter the rest of heaven after he had finished the labours of earth. We are prone, in dwelling on the character of our Lord, to overlook the fact that he was truly man, in contemplating the fact that he was truly God. As man, he had all the feelings of a sinless humanity. He could be touched with a feeling of all our infirmities that were without sin. He was weary, hungry, thirsty, faint, lonely, sorrowful, indignant, as he encountered the various trials of his earthly life. Hence, even without any specific assurances, we would have inferred that he felt the same longing for heaven that the lonely and weary often have on earth. But we have assurances most explicitly given. Paul declares to us that he, *"for the joy that was set before him,* endured the cross, despising the shame, and is set down at the right hand of the throne of God." Heb. 12.2. Hence, this Ascension or return to heaven was a thing that cheered and sustained him in his sorrows on earth. To him the hope of heaven was something far more vivid and bright then to any other soul that has ever longed for it. We know not how far the consciousness of the humanity shared the knowledge of the Divinity, but we know that there was some impartation of that knowledge. "What and if ye shall see the Son of man ascend up where he was before?" (John 6.62) was a question that indicated this fact. But it was yet more touchingly declared in the intercessory prayer in the seventeenth chapter of John's Gospel. The whole prayer breathes the home-sick longing of a child for his Father's house, and a soul ripe for heaven yearning for its rest. Take, for example, the unutterable tenderness of the heart-gushing words, "I have glorified thee on the earth: I have finished the work which thou gavest me to do. And now, O Father, glorify thou me with thine own

self, with the glory which I had with thee before the world was." John 17.4, 5. There is a wonderful depth of beauty and tenderness in these words. They are the longing of a weary heart that is conscious of having faithfully done its work, and now wistfully looks for its release and repose. We cannot doubt that to the lonely man of sorrows there came visions of the better land, memories of the sweet rest above, echoings of the minstrelsy of the heavenly harps, whisperings of angels, and thoughts of the city that hath foundations, and the home and the throne that awaited him, such as none other ever had, and such as none other ever needed. As he trod the dusty streets of the cities of Palestine, laid his head beneath the lowly roof of Bethlehem, spent the long cold night on the mountain-top and the sea-shore, we are assured by these words of Paul that his eye was often lifted to the everlasting hills, gazing on the throne that glittered there in reserve for him in the land that was afar off. These hopes cheered him in his toils and sorrows.

Now, to a holy being, toiling on earth, it was needful that when this work was done he should return to that holy city and holy company that awaited him above. Heaven is the great gathering-place of all that is holy, and lovely, and grand in the universe; and by its mighty magnetism is drawing to it all that is loveliest and purest in creation, and clustering it in a bright eternal harmony around the throne. Hence, had Jesus been only a mere and ordinary creature, it would have been a fitting thing for him to ascend to this glorious rest when his work was done. But he was not such a creature. He was the second Adam, the representative of redeemed humanity, and as such, it was needful for him to enter paradise regained, as our forerunner. And to show that heaven was a place as well as a state, and that he was the Saviour of the body as well as of the soul, it was needful that he should go up in his human body, and enter the heavenly city as our great Leader, take possession of it in our name, and thus give us assurance that the body as well as the soul should be saved; and therefore that there should be hereafter a resurrection from the dead in glory of all who sleep in Jesus.

The great fact of instruction and comfort to us, then, in the Ascension of our Lord, is, that it is at once the pledge and the picture of our future glory as Christians. The fact that it was the same body which died that also arose and ascended to heaven, is an assurance to us that the same body that we carry about us in our earthly pilgrimage shall be taken hereafter to heaven, and that this vile body shall be made like to Christ's glorious body. As he ascended, so also shall we. As he lingered, after his new life, for forty days on earth, and then went up to heaven, so shall we, even after our new life, our spiritual resurrection, linger for a time on earth, and then ascend to heaven, first, in our disembodied spirits at death, and afterwards, in both body and spirit, hereafter, at the resurrection and second coming of Jesus. Hence, death is not a descent into the grave to the Christian, but an ascension to heaven. It is a going up to Jesus, an entrance into the heavenly city; and as our risen bodies shall be caught up to meet the Lord in the air at the Resurrection, so at death we shall be conveyed by angels to our rest, and shall see the everlasting doors lifted up to welcome us home to the King of glory.

(8) Another reason is found in the fact, that as *Mediatorial King, he was to "sit on the right hand of God."* This expression is of course not to be taken literally, as God has neither right nor left hand, as a literal fact. To sit on the right hand is to occupy a place of the highest confidence and authority, and when spoken of a king, in oriental idiom, means to share his royal authority. In regard to the Person of Christ, it means that he was to have the highest majesty and glory placed upon it, and that it was to be invested with universal dominion. This glory and dominion could not be enjoyed if he remained on earth, and hence to enter upon them it was needful that he should ascend to heaven. The kingdom here

alluded to is that mediatorial kingdom, spoken of by Paul in 1
Cor. 15.24-28, which the Son shall deliver to the Father when
the end shall come. It was to this he also alluded when he said
to his disciples, "If ye loved me ye would rejoice because I
said, I go unto the Father, for my Father is greater than I."
John 14.28. The fact that he was to ascend to the right hand
of the Father was a ground of rejoicing, not only on his
account, but on ours also. He is not only unutterably glorious
and happy in heaven, but he is dispensing the government of
the universe, so that all things work together for the glory of
his church. This kingly rule of Jesus, the Mediator, is a sheet-
anchor of hope in the darkest hour, for we know that with
Christ in the vessel we need not fear the storm.

Hence we see how full of instruction, comfort, and joy is
the great fact of the Ascension. It is an opening of the golden
gates, and the nearest approach to a visible unveiling of its
glories that shall be given until the everlasting gates shall be
lifted up, not to welcome the King of glory back, but to return
him, in all the pomp of the second advent, to judge the world.
As we gaze on the sky that was once opened by the receding
form of our blessed Lord, we may feel as the immortal
dreamer in his vision, as he looked after the entering pilgrims.
"I beheld the golden streets, and the men with crowns on
heads, and palms in their hands, and golden harps to sing
praises withal." "And after that, they shut up the gates;
which when I had seen, I wished myself among them." Then
let the Ascension of Jesus draw our thoughts, affections and
longings more to the rest that remaineth for his people.

CHAPTER 20

THE PARTING PROMISE

The lingering benediction. I. *The appearance of the Angels.* Angelic agency—Its reality and blessedness—Its nature. II. The *Angelic Message.* (1) The rebuke—Gazing too long into heaven—"Oh! to be wi' thee, Richie!"—Pining sinfully for heaven. (2) The comfort—"This same Jesus"—The unchanging Friend. (3) The warning—The second coming of Christ—The Old Testament Prophets—The New Testament Prophets—Why such obscurity around the time and manner of this coming—The great Epiphany—Conclusion—The fulness of instruction during the forty days—The coming Era—Signs of the times—The Pentecost of the future.

"We must not stand to gaze too long,
  Though on unfolding heaven our gaze we bend;
When lost behind the bright angelic throng,
  We see Christ's entering triumph slow ascend.
No fear but we shall soon behold,
  Faster than now it fades, that gleam revive,
When issuing from his cloud of fiery gold,
  Our wasted frames feel the true sun and live.
Then shall we see thee as thou art,
  For ever fixed in no unfruitful gaze,
But such as lifts the new created heart
  Age after age in worthier love and praise."

"And while they looked steadfastly toward heaven, as he went up, behold, two men stood by them in white apparel; which also said, Ye men of Galilee, why stand ye gazing up into heaven? This same Jesus which is taken up from you into heaven, shall so come in like manner as ye have seen him go into heaven."—Acts 1.10, 11.

We have been looking at the appearances of our Lord, and learning the lessons they are designed to teach. We now reach his disappearance, and the lessons that we are to learn from that great fact. And it has been kindly ordered by our Master that these lessons should not be left to mere conjecture. We have them uttered to us by the lips of angels, and thus taught in the most impressive manner.

It was a touching fact that, in the Ascension, the Saviour was taken up in the very act of blessing his disciples. The benediction was begun on earth, but not ended, for "while he blessed them, he was parted from them, and carried up into heaven." That benediction still lingers in the air, and cheers the hearts of Christ's people, and will continue to do so, until the words of the departing Saviour are swallowed up in the sounds that shall proclaim the coming Judge.

It was most natural that the disciples should continue to gaze at the receding cloud of light that enfolded the form of their beloved Master. They were moved with mingled emotions of amazement, sorrow, longing, and fear. They felt that they were now really alone, and the first feeling of their hearts would be that of Elisha, when he witnessed the ascension of Elijah: "My father, my father, the chariots of Israel and the horsemen thereof." Like him they must have felt that their great protection and guidance was gone in his removal, and had nothing more been said, they would probably have returned to the city with doubting and sorrowful hearts. But they were not so to be left, for as they gazed up into heaven, there appeared two forms above them clad in the garb of heavenly messengers, who gently reproved their doubting sorrow, and gave them the assurance that this departing Saviour should come again, and close up the great mystery of God, in the sublime scenes of the last great day. There are several things here that strike us: first, the appearance of the angels, and then the message they delivered.

1. *The Appearance of the angels.*

It is a striking fact that this wonderful interval in our Lord's life, was introduced and closed by appearances of angels. The Resurrection was announced by angels at the threshold of the grave, the second advent was announced by angels at the gates of heaven. They came as heralds to proclaim his coming from death, they remained as heralds to proclaim his coming to judgment. Thus the gloom of the grave, and the pains of parting, are both lightened to the hearts of the disciples by the words of angels. And it is a thought not sufficiently pondered, that the last words that fell on the ears of the disciples at this memorable time were the words of angels.

The instructive fact presented to us here is, that angelic interposition was made at the very time when it was most needed. When our Lord was visibly present with his disciples, they needed no special comfort. But when he had left them alone, their hearts were ready to sink, and they needed consolation. Hence he sent angels to them not to declare any new truth to them, but only to remind them of the old, and to recall to them those familiar things which, in their bewildered amazement, they had been unable to remember.

Thus it is that God always deals with his people. If he takes away one comfort, he puts another in its place, more suitable for our circumstances, all things considered, than that which was taken. And more than this, it is further true, that God often uses the very same agency now that he did then on Olivet.

Angelic agency is a topic from which the pulpit perhaps shrinks unduly. There is a temptation to give loose to fancy that makes many avoid it, lest the simple and sober statement of the truth should be regarded as fanciful. And there is also a secret scepticism in regard to the real existence of such agency now, that perhaps has more to do with our silence on the subject than we would willingly confess. We may not doubt it ourselves, but the fact that it is doubted by many others, causes ministers often to shrink from declaring the whole truth on this subject. Yet no fact is more clearly revealed than this very agency. They are ministering spirits sent forth to minister to the heirs of salvation. They bear us up in their hands, lest we dash our foot against a stone. Their busy activity, behind the materialism of the outward and visible agencies of nature, is distinctly and repeatedly taught. Why should we forget or conceal it? Why not take the comfort it is designed to give us? Why not cherish the hallowing restraint and check it is calculated to throw around us? We know how the presence of a fellow man comforts, restrains, and assists us, if he is a man of holy and elevated character. And ought not the presence of angels to have the same effect? When we sit in our lonely dwelling or walk in the pathway of sorrow, ought not angelic presences to cheer and brighten our souls? When we are tempted to sin, ought not the thought that there perhaps then rests upon us the sorrowful eye of an angel, to aid in restraining us? Yet all this is undoubted fact. It is no dream of poetic fancy, but the simple verity of revelation that these unseen agencies are ever around us. Paul enjoined a decent conformity to established notions of propriety in public assemblies, because of the presence of angels in them. He himself was visited on the stormy Adriatic, and comforted by an angel. Peter was released by the hands of an angel. The angel of the Lord encamps around the pillow of his suffering people, and makes all their bed in their sickness. When a single sinner repents, there is joy among them. And when the weary task of life is done, though the saint be a beggar at the gate of unfeeling opulence, he is carried by the angels into Abraham's bosom.

But what is the nature of this agency? Is it miraculous? Is it designed to give any new revelations? By no means. It is simply to do as the angels did on Olivet, remind us of the words of Jesus. This is all we need to comfort us, for it carries us above angelic agency to him who is the Lord of angels. We know not how often the dropping of some sweet text into the soul, that falls softly like a voice from heaven on the fainting heart, is the whispering agency of one of these unseen remembrancers. They too worship Jesus, and though they cannot unite in that richer, deeper song, that is sung by the ransomed sinner, "to him that loved us, and washed us from our sins in his own blood;" yet they may unite in that other song that ascribes honour, glory, praise, and power, to him that sits upon the throne and to the Lamb for ever. And it is this adoring love of Jesus that leads them to such ministries of affection as they are ever performing for his people. Hence the appearance of these angels at this time, when the disciples so much needed their comfort, was simply an instance of a general law still in operation.

2. *The Angelic Message.*

"Ye men of Galilee, why stand ye gazing up into heaven? This same Jesus which is taken up from you into heaven, shall so come in like manner as ye have seen him go into heaven." This message contains words of rebuke, of comfort, and of warning.

(1) *The rebuke.* The interrogatory of the angels certainly conveys a gentle, but yet a decided reproof. "Why stand ye gazing up into heaven?" The feeling here rebuked was one with which every mourner is sadly familiar. When the gates of heaven have opened to admit some dear one taken from our side, what is the feeling that first springs up in the heart? Is it not a wistful longing to follow them? Is it not a feeling that the earth is too dark and cold now, for us to remain here? Is it not a gazing up into heaven with a feeling almost of impatience at the obstacles that prevent us from going there?

It is touchingly told of Alexander Peden, that when hunted by the dragoons of Claverhouse, and compelled to hide in dens and caves of the earth, he was accustomed to steal at times to the grave of Richard Cameron, at Airsmoss, and as he thought of the harassing sorrows of earth, and the sweet rest of heaven into which his martyred brother had entered, he would exclaim with a bursting heart and a streaming eye, "Oh! to be wi' thee, Richie!" This is a feeling that strong hearts have often had in an hour of sorrow. When Jonah found that his expectations in regard to the glory of his own people, and the punishment of their enemies, were to be disappointed, he went out of Nineveh, and longed to die. And when Elijah fled from Jezebel into the wilderness, thinking that all was lost, and that God's cause was crushed hopelessly, he also lay down beneath a juniper tree and longed for death. The same thing was true of Moses in the moment of discouragement. And thus it is often with stricken hearts in the first hours of bereavement and suffering. They gaze wistfully into heaven, longing to escape from the toils, and sorrows, and loneliness of earth, and like David, take the wings of a dove, and fly away and be at rest from the windy storm and tempest.

When these seasons of depression come upon us, then should we listen to the lesson contained in these gently rebuking words of the angels: Why this gazing?

To the hearts of the disciples these words conveyed a great deal. They said to them, "Why thus long to escape from toil and trial? Return to Jerusalem and you shall in due time receive the promise of the Father, and then go and labour to the ends of the earth. Gird yourselves to obey the parting words of your Lord, and patiently wait until he fulfils his promise. He has said, 'I go to prepare a place for you, and if I go and prepare a place for you, I will come again and receive you to myself'; and will he not come? Then do not cherish these desponding feelings. Gaze not with this wistful longing at the pearly gates, and the heavenly city. The time has not come for you to enter them. It is yours to work and wait, and they will be richer and brighter to you when you reach them by reason of this very waiting." The same lesson is conveyed to us now. We must patiently labour, and patiently wait; and the rest will grow sweeter as we thus wait, and the reward will grow richer as we thus labour.

That this rebuke had its proper effect in the case of the disciples, we see from the fact that they returned to Jerusalem with "great joy." They were still alone, their beloved Master in heaven, but they knew that he had gone to prepare a place for them, that their parting was but for a time, their meeting would be for eternity; and that in a little while they would all meet in that general assembly and church of the first born, where their light affliction, that is but for a moment, shall work out a far more exceeding and eternal weight of glory.

The same lesson also should be learned by us in our hours of sorrow and discouragement. When longings for heaven unfit us for labours on earth, a voice from heaven should come, in gentle rebuke, "Why stand ye gazing up into heaven?" Instead of indolently longing for the rest of heaven, we should labour on earth to be fitted for that rest, and thus only shall we long aright. We may gaze upward toward the heavenly hills in faith and hope, and with such longings as Paul had when he was willing rather to depart and be with Christ, which was far better. But we are not to gaze with impatient discontent, and indolent desire to escape from the duties that God has assigned us here on earth. We must feel with Job, not when he exclaims in bitterness, "I loathe it; I would not live alway," but rather when he says, "All the days of my appointed time will I wait, till my change come." Job 7. 16; 14. 14.

(2) *The comfort.* "This same Jesus which is taken up from you into heaven, shall so come in like manner as ye have seen him go into heaven."

When we part with a friend who is going to scenes more attractive than those he leaves behind, we often fear lest the change of scene shall produce a change of feeling, and we be forgotten. Such changes often happen on earth. Those whom we have known in youth, we find to have grown cold in maturer years; those who have smiled upon us in prosperity and gladness, forsake us in adversity, poverty, and sorrow. To feel the chill of this change falling on our hearts, is one of the saddest experiences of life. It may be that such was the feeling of the disciples, as they saw Jesus ascend in glory. They feared lest he would not be the same loving and lowly one to them in heaven, that he had been on earth.

But it was otherwise with Jesus. He was unchangeable, so completely so, that when he would return the second time in the pomp of judgment, it would be "this *same* Jesus" who would return unchanged in all the lovely and gentle traits of his nature. The heavens shall pass away like a scroll, and the earth be burned up, but he shall remain the same, yesterday, to-day, and for ever. This is a precious truth in a world of change and uncertainty. All around us is changing. Society changes from year to year by death and removal. We ourselves change continually from youth to age, in all that pertains to us. All around us is subject to this great law of change, and there is no sure basis of hope in life. But we have to do with a Saviour who is unchanging and unchangeable. That same Jesus who spake kindly to the widow of Nain, and the sisters of Bethany, in their hour of bereavement; who gave peace to the afflicted hearts of his disciples in the midnight storm of Gennesaret; who wept over Jerusalem in gushing tenderness and regret; who wrestled in agony in Gethsemane; and prayed for his enemies on Calvary; that same Jesus still sits on the throne of glory above and is yet touched with a feeling of our infirmities, and can sympathize with us in all our sorrows, and have a fellow-feeling in our infirmities. This is a thought full of sweetness to us amid the trials of life, and the fears of death and judgment. That same Jesus who has supported others, will support us, if we trust him, and keep what we commit to him "until that day."

(3) *The Warning.* "This same Jesus . . . shall come."

The great event here predicted is the second coming of Christ. This event has been the great burden of prophecy, since the entrance of sin into the world. Enoch looked forward to it and declared that "the Lord cometh with ten thousands of his saints, to execute judgment upon all." Jude 14, 15. Job looked forward to it as he expected his Redeemer to stand at the latter day upon the earth. David expected it as he declared, "Our Lord shall come and not keep silence, a fire shall devour before him, it shall be very tempestuous round about him. He shall call to the heavens from above, and to the earth, that he may judge his people." Psalm 50. 3, 4. Isaiah, Jeremiah, Ezekiel, and Daniel, all had glimpses of this mighty event, and kindled into rapture as they looked forward to it. Joel spake of the coming of "the great and terrible day of the Lord," "the day of the Lord in the valley of decision." Joel 2. 31; 3. 14. Habakkuk seems to have written his sublime ode of a coming God, in the light of this awful day. Haggai and Zechariah looked forward to it, as they linked this day with the work of rearing from the dust, the temple, that earthly symbol of great heavenly realities. And as the spirit of prophecy was about to withdraw for a time from the church, Malachi gazes on it with the most intense emotion, and exclaims, "The day! it comes! burning as an oven! The great and dreadful day of the Lord!" The last ray that fell on the eye of prophecy as the curtain fell, was the red glare of this coming of the Lord.

When we open the New Testament these warnings become more distinct and emphatic. Our Lord himself repeatedly speaks of the coming of the Son of Man. He compares that coming, as to its suddenness and fearfulness, to the days of Noah and of Lot, when the flood and the fire from heaven swept away the ungodly. He compares it to the sudden flashing of the lightning, whose outburst can never be foreseen. He warns his his disciples that they should live with their loins girded, waiting for the coming of the Son of man. Some of his most solemn parables, those of the Virgins and Talents especially, are based on this dread coming. And among the last and most awful pictures that he gave of the future, that sublime scene in which he would separate an assembled world as the shepherd divides his sheep from his goats, his coming is the dread theme on which he speaks.

The apostles take up the same note of warning. As soon as Peter opened the gospel to the multitudes on the day of pentecost, he pointed forward to this coming as the restitution of all things spoken of by the holy prophets, since the world began. Paul repeats the warning in nearly all his epistles. In the very first one he wrote, that to Thessalonica, he dwells so repeatedly on this theme that his words were misapprehended, and it was needful for him to write a second letter, and assure them that in dwelling so much on this great coming he did not mean to represent it as at hand, for there were many great events that must previously happen. But both these early epistles dwell with great earnestness and beauty on this coming of the Lord. Nor were these merely his early and immature opinions. As he writes to the Corinthians in the noonday of his laborious career he still points them in both his letters to this great event, linking even the Lord's supper with it, as a showing of the Lord's death until he come. Nor did he think less of it toward the close of his life. As he writes to his beloved Philippians, he speaks exultingly of his looking for Jesus again from heaven to change this vile body to the likeness of his glorious body. In writing to the Colossians, he also points to the appearance of Christ in glory, and in the epistles to Timothy and Titus frequently refers to this blessed hope, the glorious appearing of the great God and our Saviour Jesus Christ. In that to the Hebrews he also speaks of his coming the second time, without sin to salvation.

Nor is this peculiar to Paul. James also warns his brethren that "the coming of our Lord draweth nigh." Peter devotes the last chapter of his second epistle, written very near to his death, to this sublime theme. Jude repeats the same things, almost in the same words. John, in his first epistle, refers repeatedly to the time when Christ should appear. The Apocalypse opens with the startling call, "Behold he cometh with clouds, and every eye shall see him," details in the most vivid manner the terrible pomp of his coming, and closes up the words of inspiration with the words of Jesus, "Surely I come quickly: Amen," and the longing prayer of the widowed and waiting church, "Even so, come, Lord Jesus."

Hence, the second coming of Christ has a place in the Scriptures, which perhaps it has not in the faith and hopes of the church. The extravagances that have often been connected with this subject in the past, have led many sober-minded Christians to submerge it in their general current of thought, and remove it from the place that it really holds in the Word of God. There are also serious differences of opinion in regard to the time, the mode, the nature, and the purpose of this coming, that even now separate the wisest and best men in every branch of the visible church. It would be aside from our present purpose even to express an opinion in regard to these disputed points, and hence we allude to them only for a specific reason.

Why is so important an event declared in such a way, that for ages, if not from the beginning, there have been differences of opinion as to its time and manner? Why are not these things as explicitly revealed as the event itself? For the very reason, that the event is to be the great lode star of the church's future in every age. Were it revealed with such absolute clearness as to time, circumstances, and manner, that its chronology could be calculated, it could never be what it was designed to be, the great awakener of the militant church. It is to be to the collective body of Christians, what the close of life is to the individual Christian, the great spur and stimulus to activity. Hence, like it, the event is certain, the time and manner uncertain; that the certainty might cause us to work because the night cometh, and that the uncertainty might cause us to work while it is called to-day. Hence, to each age this event stands at once a near and a remote event: near, if measured by the standard of heaven, remote, if by that of earth; but in either case the great, decisive event of the future, that for which the church in the wilderness below, and the souls beneath the altar above, have been crying, "How long, O Lord?" and for which a travailing creation has been waiting for the glorious manifestation of the sons of God.

This only we need know, that "this same Jesus" shall so come in like manner as he was seen to go into heaven. This *same* Jesus, who having loved his own, loved them to the end; who having loved them on earth, will continue to love them in heaven. He shall *so* come as he was seen to go into heaven; not figuratively, but literally; not spiritually, but bodily; not to the eye of faith alone, but visibly; not in the presence of a few angels and a handful of disciples, but with "the ten thousand times ten thousand," when every eye shall see him, and all the kindreds of the earth shall wail because of him. He shall come to make that "restitution of all things spoken of by the mouth of all his holy prophets since the world began." He shall come "to judge the world in righteousness," and "render to every man according to his deeds; to them who by patient continuance in well-doing, seek for glory, and honour, and immortality, eternal life: but unto them that are contentious, and do not obey the truth, but obey unrighteousness, indignation and wrath, tribulation and anguish, upon every soul of man that doeth evil." He shall come to say to those on his right hand, "Come, ye blessed of my Father, inherit the kingdom prepared for you from the foundation of the world."

Hence this great event is the goal of the church's race; the triumphal end of her long warfare; the welcome home of her weary pilgrimage; the termination of her life militant; the beginning of her life triumphant. We can thus readily see why it is called "a glorious hope," and why it hung gleaming on the horizon of the church's hope in the days of her early struggles, as the bright Epiphany whose full appearance would compensate for all the sore strugglings of the sorrowful and darkened past and present.

To the individual Christian it comes also with the same high power to comfort and arouse. It is true that to him death is nearer, in all human probability, than this great day, but death itself has all its dread or glad significance from its connection with this great appearing. To us all, practically, the coming of death is the coming of judgment, for what is left undone at the one event, shall be found undone at the other. Hence for the same reason that the church is called to wait and to watch, in hope, in activity, and in submission, the individual Christian also is called to wait and to watch, that whenever the great messenger Death shall come, he may be found ready to go into the presence of the great Master with joy, and not with grief.

Hence, as the disciples returned to Jerusalem from Olivet with great joy, and waited for the promise of the Lord, in prayer, in faith, and in the discharge of duty, so should it be with the individual Christian after every visit to Olivet; after every opening of heaven to admit an ascending spirit; after every season of instruction, of discipline, or of trial. He should gird himself afresh for the duties and difficulties of the present, by the hope that he has of the glorious revelations of the future. Thus let each one strive to live more constantly in the light of the great Epiphany of the future—

> "The bright appearance of the Lord,
> While faith stands leaning on his Word."

We have now gone over the appearances of our Lord during the memorable Forty Days, and have found them rich in instruction to a very remarkable degree. There is hardly a leading doctrine in the Christian system that was not in some form brought forward during these memorable interviews. There is hardly a phase of Christian experience that is not brought into review in the words spoken by our Lord during this remarkable period. It was, therefore, to the apostles, a season of training, that fitted them eminently for the great work to which they were called in preaching the gospel to all nations. Like the forty days that preceded the public ministry of our Lord, it was designed and adapted in an eminent degree to furnish preparation for the new manifestation of the kingdom then to be made.

We are standing now apparently at the dawn of a new era in the great work of Redemption. All the lines of prophecy, chronological and historical, seem to centre in the quarter of a century on which we are now entering. The whole world, especially Europe and Asia, seems heaving with internal elements of convulsion, as if preparing for some fearful outburst that shall shatter the ancient crust that has been petrifying for ages; the shattering of which must bring about some new form of social and political, if not religious development. There is a restless uneasiness with the present, and an anxious looking to the future, which recalls the words of Jesus that a time would come when "men's hearts would be failing them for fear, and for looking after those things which are coming on the earth." There is a vast increase of all kinds of material facilities, and improvements, such as preceded and prepared the way for the great Reformation of the sixteenth century. There is an increasing sense of responsibility on the part of the Church, a multiplication of modes of active labour in Christ's cause, that looks like a preparation of agencies for action, that shall be ready when the call comes for their use. Every thing betokens some new manifestation of the kingdom of Christ. What this shall be, we know not. Whether a single advance of the same kind with those that have preceded it, or a mightier and more stupendous revealing of himself, we cannot tell. But in any case, it becomes us to fill our vessels, and trim our lamps, and gird our loins, and look out on the still night around us, remembering that "the night is far spent and the day is at hand," and "now is our salvation nearer than when we believed." And there is no portion of Scripture which we can more fitly study than that which records the teachings of that memorable Forty Days which preceded the great outpouring of the Spirit, and the inauguration of the New Testament form of the kingdom of heaven. Let us then ponder, and watch, and pray, and labour, and then patiently wait, and perhaps we may soon see the descending tokens of fire from heaven that shall announce the advent of the mighty pentecost of the future. "Behold I come quickly. Amen. Even so come, Lord Jesus. The grace of our Lord Jesus Christ be with you all. Amen."